CONTENTS

FLAT-TOP and RATCHET by SCHOFIELD ©98

PRACTICAL HOT RODDER'S GUIDE

chopping
TOPS

LARRY O'TOOLE

GRAFFITI

Published in 2000 by

Graffiti Publications Pty. Ltd.,

69 Forest Street, Castlemaine, Victoria, Australia

Phone International 61 3 5472 3653

Fax International 61 3 5472 3805

Email: graffiti@netcon.net.au

Website: www.graffitipub.com.au

Copyright 2000 by Larry O'Toole

Design: Michael deWolfe

Illustration: Alan Schofield

Colour Separations: Sharpscan, West Melbourne

Printing: Centre State Printing, Maryborough

The information in this book is true and complete to the best of our knowledge. All recommendations are made without any guarantee on the part of the author or publisher, who also disclaim any liability incurred in connection with the use of this data or specific details.

We recognise that some words, model names and designations mentioned herein are the property of the trademark holder. We use them for identification purposes only. This is not an official publication.

Graffiti Publications books are also available at discounts in bulk quantity for industrial or sales promotional use.

For details contact Graffiti Publications Ph: (613) 5472 3653

Printed and bound in Australia.

ISBN 0 949398 18 7

Larry O'Toole

CHOPPING THE TOP OF A VEHICLE IS THE ONE MAJOR custom body modifications that has always been seen as the ultimate styling change. It is a radical procedure. To actually remove the roof of an automobile, eliminate part of the supporting structures and then replace the roof is no small operation. It is also an operation that could seriously jeopardise the strength and integrity of the vehicle if this type of modification is done badly. The purpose of this book is to help you understand and undertake a top chopping operation in the best way possible.

Every vehicle that you might attempt to chop is going to be different. The design of the roof and the way it attaches to the main vehicle structure varies greatly from one automobile to another and from one time period to another. Generally speaking early vehicles that might be subjected to top chopping are easier than later models. Hot rods based on late 1920s to mid-1930s vehicles are usually the easiest to chop because for the most part they have straight, upright pillars and relatively square window openings. From about 1935 onwards the windshield pillars were gradually laid back more and window openings started to take on more rounded shapes. Move up to the mid-fifties and we encounter the introduction of wrap around windshields, further complicating matters, particularly when it comes to modifying the windshield glass.

There are examples of all these types of vehicles from all these eras within the pages of this book. Hopefully the methods shown will be a significant help when you attempt your own top chopping project. But there will always be something you hadn't bargained for in your particular case. That's part of the game, I'm afraid, and no book will ever be able to answer every question completely. However I trust that you will be better armed to undertake your own top chop after reading this book. There is just one suggestion that I would make when it comes to the hard part of any top chopping operation. Think first, act later!

The most important part of chopping a top is the very first step in the process. That is to ponder the operation deeply, think through all the ramifications of the options before you start, and don't cut anything until you are absolutely sure everything is right. If you undertake this process thoroughly you may spend as much time thinking through all the possibilities as you will actually cutting and welding. Of course once you have the thought process under control you will then have to spend many hours with tape measure in hand checking that all your options will work and marking out the roof in preparation for the chopping to commence.

My own approach to chopping a top is to use the methods just described, but even when I have the vehicle entirely marked out ready for cutting I then prefer to walk away. It is very easy to overlook something that could be important as the chop progresses. I like to leave the whole vehicle marked out but left untouched for at least one night, then start cutting in the morning. Often you will find that some adjustment needs to be made before you start cutting. I have used this process on many occasions and in some instances it has saved hours of extra work.

Why would just thinking about how you will chop a top need to take up so much time? Well there is a lot to contemplate, especially with later model vehicles where angles can get very complex. The shape of the window openings, the slant of the pillars, even the shape of the turret itself will all play a part in your decision making process as to which way is best to chop this particular vehicle. Often the roof will need to be split in several locations to allow the pillars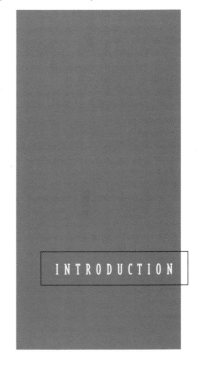

INTRODUCTION

to align in their new positions. Sometimes you can 'cheat' by leaning a pillar that was straight originally or by moving the entire roof forwards or backwards to make alignment easier. All these things need to float through your mind as you contemplate the project.

Once you complete this phase you can start measuring and marking out the top ready for cutting. If you have been successful in thinking through the process properly you may have some unusual sections marked out. Pillars won't necessarily be marked for cutting somewhere near the middle. Window shape, hardware location and even rubber insulators may dictate that a cut needs to be relocated from where you might have first considered making it. You may even find that the cut on the outside of a pillar will need to be different to the inside.

Wherever the pillar cuts are made there is one very important consideration to keep in mind. That is to ensure the strength and integrity of the vehicle isn't compromised by your modifications. You may need to reinforce pillars with additional steel inserts or you may need to cut away small sections of external sheet metal to allow access to an inner pillar for welding.

Another practical addition you can make to many early model vehicles while you are in the process of chopping the pillars is to include steel inserts for upper seat belt mounts. You shouldn't only look to preserve the integrity of the original vehicle; you might as well improve its safety at the same time. Plan accordingly.

It still isn't time to start cutting yet. Part of the exercise in maintaining the integrity of the original vehicle is to ensure that everything stays in alignment while you cut the thing into pieces. That will require some more planning.

The first step is to jack the vehicle clear of the floor, or at least until the suspension is no longer supporting the weight of the vehicle. Next it should be supported with solid stands at several points so that there isn't any opportunity for the chassis or subframes to flex once the support of the roof is removed.

Removing the roof will allow the remaining body sections to move all over the place as the floor will then be the only thing holding them all together, so we need to add reinforcement to keep them in alignment too. This is usually done by building a steel framework within the body as close to the belt-line as possible. There are a couple of examples contained within this book but usually such a frame would consist of a pair of substantial rails down the inside of the vehicle with cross braces attached to hold everything in place. Bolting in steel members from door latch to hinge holes will maintain the door openings in relation to each other and cross braces welded from these to the inner frame members will maintain side to side alignment. Substantial tack welding of this entire framework is all that is required. As long as they won't break while you climb all over them they will do their job, and remember you will need to remove them again once the top chop is completed.

Now it is finally time to pick up your tools and start cutting! Which sections are cut off first will be largely dictated by the particular vehicle you are chopping. Your own thinking process should have resulted in you knowing that, before you begin cutting. Many tools will be required from simple hacksaws to elaborate electrical or air driven cutting tools. Use what you have or can readily borrow or hire.

When it comes time to weld it all back together there are several options again. These days many enthusiasts have both a MIG welder and a more traditional gas-welding outfit available to them. Some may even have a TIG welder but it isn't necessary for this type of work. I prefer to use a MIG welder for the parts that require heavier welding, such as the pillars and some of the internal reinforcing panels, but when it comes time to weld up the sheet metal panels I prefer oxy-acetylene welding. This leaves a softer, more diffused weld bead that is easier to work with slapping iron or hammer and dolly. The MIG tends to leave a harder deposit that is more brittle and can tend to crack when being worked with the panel beating tools. Use what suits your own requirements and skill levels.

If you aren't a proficient welder you should have someone who is experienced carry out the major welding for you, or practise on an old body that can be discarded before you undertake a major project like a top chop. For MIG welding the pillars and other heavy sections make sure the areas to be joined are as accessible and clean as possible so that you can get full penetration. Some heavy sections may even require that the edges are bevelled with a grinder to allow full penetration. Any thicker than 1/16" steel should be bevelled in this manner.

When gas welding body panels the most important consideration is to have the edges to be joined as closely matched to each other as possible. If you get this very accurate you will find that very little filler rod is required and the final welding will be very easy. Panels should be completely tack welded together every 3/4 inch or so before any final welding is undertaken. Try to minimise the use of hammer and dolly as you go. Use them to maintain alignment only with minimal tapping and bumping. The same goes for the final welding process, only use the hammer, or as I prefer, the slapping iron and dolly to keep things generally in alignment. This way you won't 'work harden' the sheet metal and when the welding is completed you will find it much easier to work the joined area back into its proper shape.

Unless you are a very skilled sheet metal worker or panel beater your basically completed top chop will be far from perfect. You will almost certainly need to perform some stretching, shrinking, filing and grinding on the roof to get it all back to its former shape and ready for paint. There are other specialist books available that can help you master these processes and they are listed at the end of this book in the 'further reading' section.

Good luck with your own top chopping project. I hope this book helps you achieve your goal.

ANYBODY CAN RESTORE A CAR, IT TAKES A
REAL MAN TO CUT ONE UP.

GUINEA PIGS FOR THESE CHOPPING OPERATIONS WERE Bill Mussett's '32 Ford three window Coupe and Noel Harper's '32 Ford Tudor. The projects called for three inches out of Bill's coupe and 2 or 2-1/2 inches from Noel's Tudor. Although both are '32 Fords there are differences between each body as the three window coupe body was made for Ford by the Murray Body Company while the Tudor was made by Ford in their own factory. While the differences might not be readily apparent to the casual viewer, apart from the fact that the three window Coupe has suicide doors, there are some important differences inside the bodies. The three window Coupe has a considerable amount of wood used to frame the inside of the body whereas the Tudor is essentially all steel. The only wood in the Tudor body is largely there to provide a basis on which to attach the interior trim.

CHAPTER ONE

There are a couple of other important differences that have a bearing on how we went about chopping each of these bodies. The three window Coupe doesn't have a drip rail above the doors while the Tudor does. There is a significant difference between the two bodies at the windshield pillar. The upper section of the door pillar on the three window Coupe body also has a forward slant which complicates the chop at this point. By comparison all of the pillars on the Tudor are relatively vertical, making them straightforward to chop.

Finally, the extra amount of wood in the three window body means that an entire new door hinge pillar was required to be made out of steel. This was completed at a later stage of the rebuild on this body and consequently isn't covered here.

It is worth noting that the chopping operations on both these bodies were carried out in the late 1970s. Bill Mussett's Coupe has been used regularly on the road ever since and still stops people in their tracks to this day. In fact our introductory photo for this chapter shows Bill's Coupe as it appears today. It is black with polished American five spoke wheels and has blown small block Chevy power under the hood.

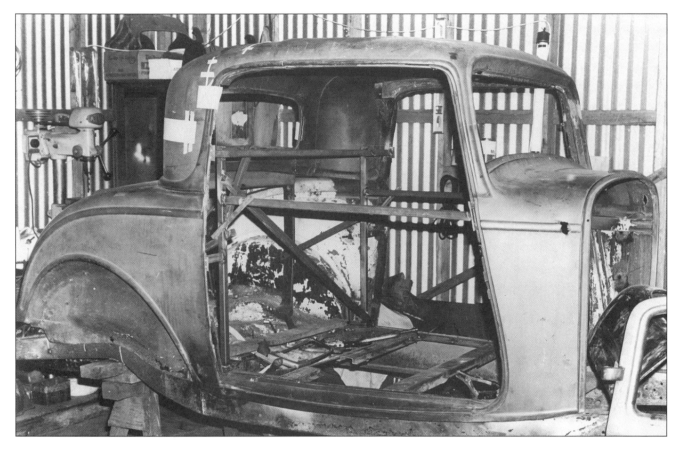

■ Compare the "before" shot above with the "after" shot below and you can appreciate the difference a top chop can make to an early Ford body. Note how the original wooden door hinge pillars have been removed but short lengths of steel are used to hold the panels in their correct position while the top chop is executed. The body is firmly bolted to the original chassis to maintain alignment.

■ Our "before" and "after" comparison shots also show how Noel's Tudor benefits from a lowered roofline. Once again the body is securely bolted in place on the chassis and an internal frame has been welded temporarily in place to keep everything in alignment while the cutting and welding proceeds. Both bodies fit to the same design firewall and chassis but are entirely different in most other respects.

■ To ensure that the body stayed in alignment this complex looking framework was made up for Bill's coupe before the chopping operation began. For the little time invested it was cheap insurance once the top was off.

■ The top was then marked out completely before any cutting took place. Note the way the cut is to be staggered near the back of the door opening. This is to maintain proper alignment of the roof around the door.

■ The windshield pillar is marked out for cutting just below the mid-point

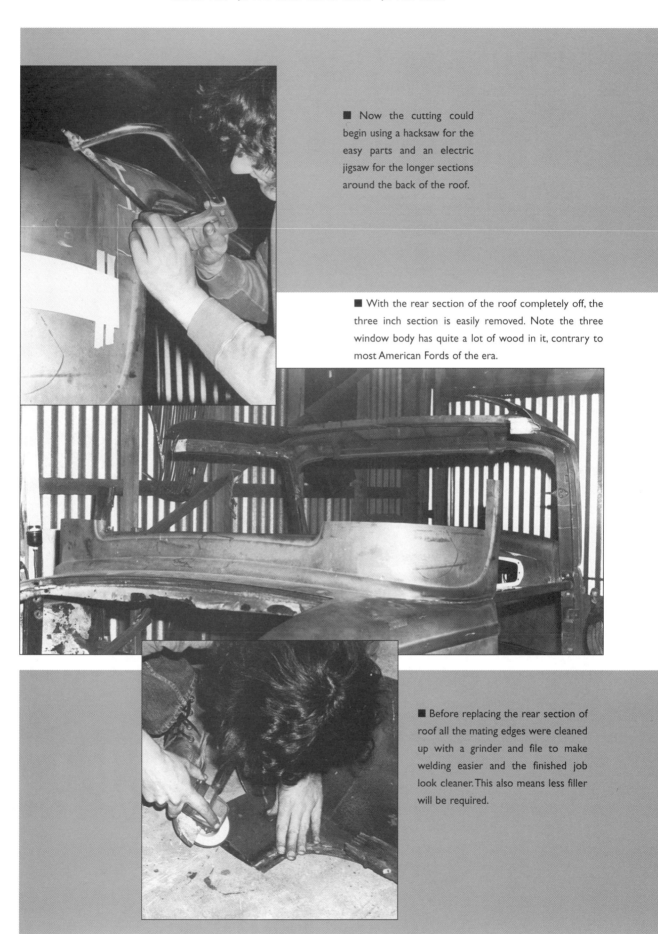

■ Now the cutting could begin using a hacksaw for the easy parts and an electric jigsaw for the longer sections around the back of the roof.

■ With the rear section of the roof completely off, the three inch section is easily removed. Note the three window body has quite a lot of wood in it, contrary to most American Fords of the era.

■ Before replacing the rear section of roof all the mating edges were cleaned up with a grinder and file to make welding easier and the finished job look cleaner. This also means less filler will be required.

■ The rear roof section is then repositioned and tacked into place before any further cutting takes place. Note however that a section of roof at the top rear corner of the doorway has been removed prior to refitting the rear portion of roof.

■ This small section is then trimmed to fit back into the rear section without altering the proportions of the door opening. Note how the curved corner of the doorway and the curves of the roofline all match up.

■ Attention turns to the front section of the roof, which is shown here sitting in place with the three-inch sections removed from the windscreen pillars. A gap of about one-inch appears in the top of the doorway at the point where the front and rear sections were separated.

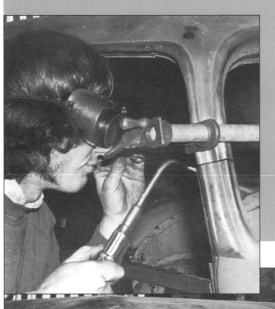

■ Despite the interior framework the windshield opening did spring apart a little when the front section of the roof was removed. A pipe clamp was employed to correct this so that alignment would be accurate. With the pipe clamp still in place the pillars were then solidly tacked into position but not finish welded until the entire roof was all one piece again.

■ The final step in this part of the operation is to fill in the gap at the top of the doorway. A piece of steel is hammer welded and worked into position and the excess trimmed off. The staggered shape of this joint is simply to make it easier to align the front and rear sections of the roof when they are tacked into position. Now that the roof is all one piece again all tacked joints can be finish welded. A new door pillar was required before work could progress any further so Bill's doors were chopped at a later date.

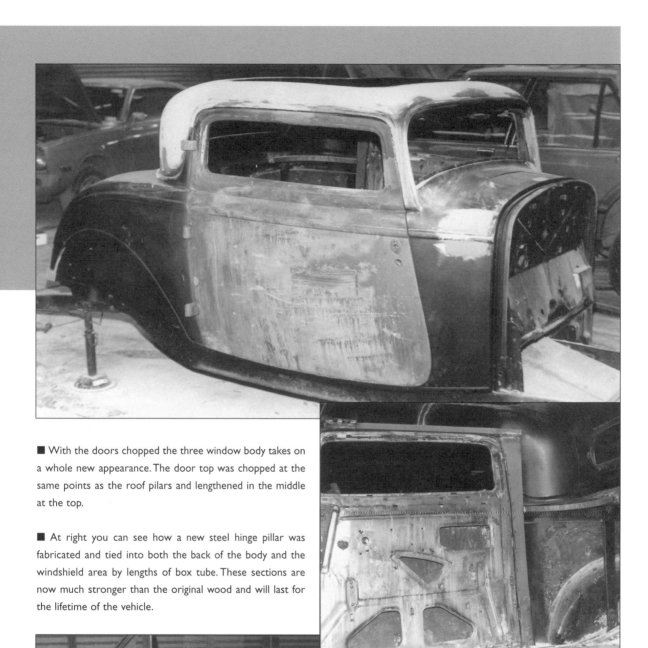

■ With the doors chopped the three window body takes on a whole new appearance. The door top was chopped at the same points as the roof pilars and lengthened in the middle at the top.

■ At right you can see how a new steel hinge pillar was fabricated and tied into both the back of the body and the windshield area by lengths of box tube. These sections are now much stronger than the original wood and will last for the lifetime of the vehicle.

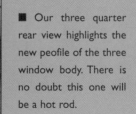

■ Our three quarter rear view highlights the new peofile of the three window body. There is no doubt this one will be a hot rod.

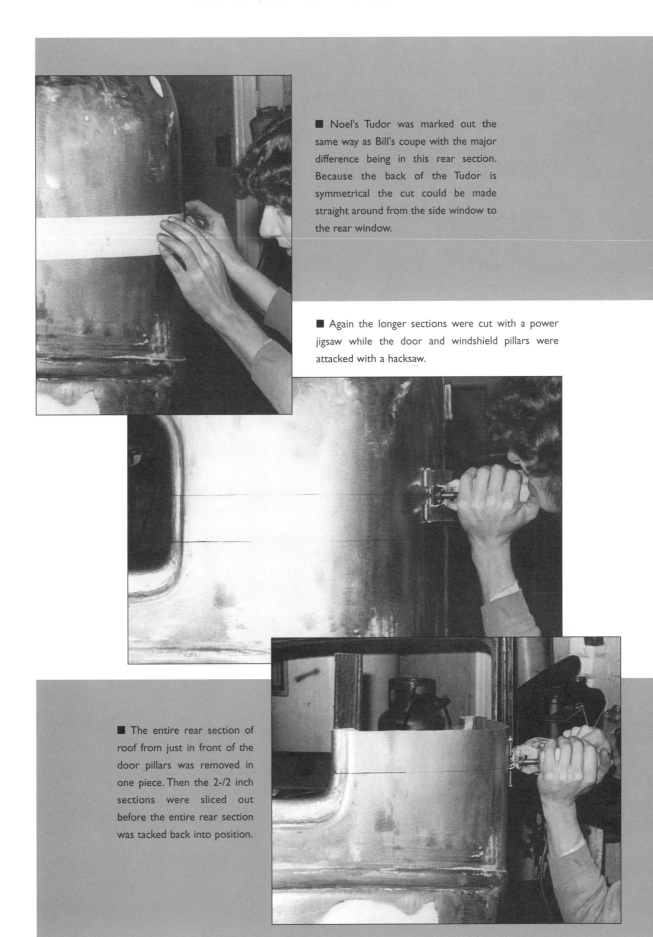

■ Noel's Tudor was marked out the same way as Bill's coupe with the major difference being in this rear section. Because the back of the Tudor is symmetrical the cut could be made straight around from the side window to the rear window.

■ Again the longer sections were cut with a power jigsaw while the door and windshield pillars were attacked with a hacksaw.

■ The entire rear section of roof from just in front of the door pillars was removed in one piece. Then the 2-/2 inch sections were sliced out before the entire rear section was tacked back into position.

■ Without further ado the front section was removed by cutting the windshield pillars near the top. Care must be used in this area on a '32 Tudor as there are many different curves, which must all be taken into consideration before the cutting is done.

■ The new roofline is readily apparent with the front section tacked back into place. Although the job looks nearly complete here the bulk of the work is still to be done.

■ Once again the cut at the top of the doorway is made in a staggered fashion to make re-alignment easy. Note that the Tudor has a drip rail whereas the three window coupe doesn't.

■ Steel strips are hammer welded into the gaps to make the roof section all one piece again. Note that a small piece of drip rail will have to be located or fabricated to fill in the gap.

■ From the inside a piece of the door pillar wood is removed to allow the pillar to be welded from the inside as well. The pillar itself is double skinned and welding both inside and out maintains the original pillar strength.

■ Most interior wood on Noel's Tudor will be replaced with steel at a later date so it was only removed where absolutely necessary during the chopping operation. All window trims were chopped in the same locations as the top.

■ To maintain alignment on the top of the door it is first chopped and then the full piece was held in position while the front end was welded in place. Then the rear half was cut off to allow for lengthening, leaving the front piece perfectly in alignment.

■ The rear piece was then securely clamped and tacked into position. Finally the gap in the middle of the door top is filled in to complete the entire chopping operation.

■ Because the front of the door tapers many different ways a compromise must be made. The inside edge is aligned to allow the window to fit as original but the outside edge must be "worked" a little and some filling will be necessary to blend all the lines together again.

■ This isn't the '32 Tudor shown in this chapter but it is chopped a similar amount and shows how dramatically a top chop changes the overall profile of a car.

CON SOLDATOS STARTED WORK ON HIS '36 FORD FIVE WINDOW COUPE back in the 1980s. Initially designed to be a radical street rod with weekend trips down the drag strip, the vehicle started out with a modified original chassis and Holden front suspension. It was very successful on the drag strips and gradually evolved into a full-on race car with tube chassis and full roll cage, strut front end and competition type four link rear suspension. Despite all these modifications the Coupe still looked like a street rod and was enormously popular on Australian and New Zealand drag strips. The car ran high eight second quarter mile times with crowd pleasing wheelstands a regular occurrence.

Con used a one-piece fiberglass front section to cover the LS 6 Chevrolet 454 engine. The big block engine was originally backed up by a Doug Nash five speed gearbox with Hurst shifter. As you see here the body was chopped two inches and extensive rust repairs carried out. The firewall was moved back approximately seven inches and made flat. Con's coupe started out to be the living image of a "full on" pro-street '36 coupe and evolved to full-on race car status over a period of years. During that time it also used several different engine combinations. Con is currently considering returning the Coupe to street rod duties.

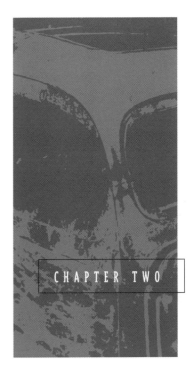

CHAPTER TWO

When the photos of the top chopping operation were taken Con's Coupe was a rusty original body in the process of being resurrected. The top chop saw two inches removed from the pillars. Like all the chopping examples shown in this book the body was securely bolted to the chassis and a frame welded into the body itself to keep everything in alignment as the work progressed.

■ Con Soldatos' '36 Ford coupe was designed to be a dual purpose street rod and race car for the drags. Despite its low stance the decision was made to chop two inches out of the roof of the coupe to maintain an overall "race" image.

The result speaks for itself. The top is now in proportion with the rest of the car but because two inches was taken out good all round vision is maintained.

■ First and most important step with any top chop is to make careful measurements and mark out the areas to be cut. Staggering the cuts as shown here makes it easy to maintain alignment as the reassembly takes place.

■ Before any cutting is done a framework is fitted inside the body which has been bolted to the chassis. The framework ties the dash to the door pillars and also cross braces the passenger area. Now the rear section of the roof is removed.

■ The two inch section is trimmed off and then the rear section is tacked back into place before any more cutting takes place. Starting like this makes alignment easier as the remaining stock height section of the roof can be used for reference. Careful measuring and cutting in the right place maintains good window shape and eliminates the need for vertical cuts to adjust alignment.

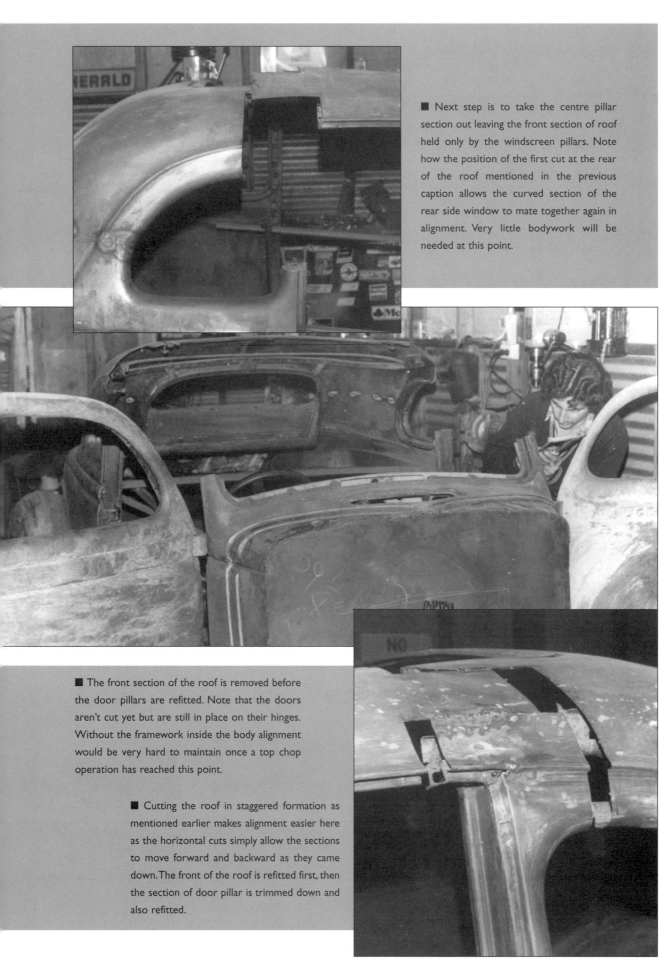

■ Next step is to take the centre pillar section out leaving the front section of roof held only by the windscreen pillars. Note how the position of the first cut at the rear of the roof mentioned in the previous caption allows the curved section of the rear side window to mate together again in alignment. Very little bodywork will be needed at this point.

■ The front section of the roof is removed before the door pillars are refitted. Note that the doors aren't cut yet but are still in place on their hinges. Without the framework inside the body alignment would be very hard to maintain once a top chop operation has reached this point.

■ Cutting the roof in staggered formation as mentioned earlier makes alignment easier here as the horizontal cuts simply allow the sections to move forward and backward as they came down. The front of the roof is refitted first, then the section of door pillar is trimmed down and also refitted.

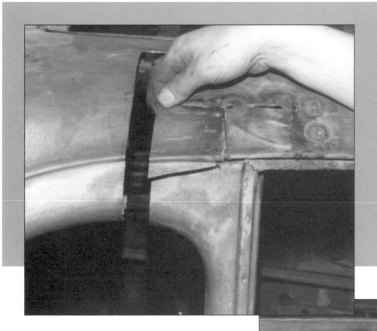

■ With the pillar section in place again we came across a minor problem. The side window alignment was correct but the lip at the edge of the roof didn't line up properly. To bring it back into line a small section was cut and moved up slightly as shown here then welded into place again.

■ Now that all alignment has been corrected all that remains in this area is to fill in the remaining gaps. This was done by hammer welding sections of sheet metal into place. The top of the door has now been cut off to allow the final stage of the cutting process to be completed.

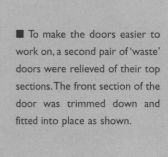

■ To make the doors easier to work on, a second pair of 'waste' doors were relieved of their top sections. The front section of the door was trimmed down and fitted into place as shown.

■ The rear section was cut in such a way that it makes up for the extra length required in the top of the door and then fitted so that only one weld is required at the top centre of the door. The 'waste' doors were off a sedan and have a slightly different curve at the top so a small amount of building up was carried out later with a MIG welder to correct a slight mismatch.

■ Now that the entire top chop is completed all sections that have been left tacked into position can be hammer welded. This is best handled by two operators one welding and the other hammering. The procedure for hammer welding is as follows; small sections about one inch long are gas welded and while still glowing red hot they are flattened with a panel beating hammer and dolly until they have stopped glowing. This is a fairly slow process but warpage is kept to an absolute minimum.

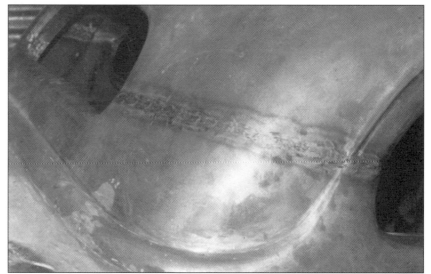

■ Once the chopping operation was completed and everything was solidly welded into place again the top inside section of the door pillars was heavily reinforced to prevent cracking. All '36 Ford coupes are prone to cracking in this area and it is hard to correct later. Then to tidy the whole area up most of the pieced together area in the roof above the door pillar was removed and replaced with one large piece of sheetmetal.

■ The finished top chop has brought the top back into proportion with the overall low stance of the car. The windshield frame is very easy to chop as it has a join at the midpoint of each side anyway. Inner window frames are treated in much the same way as the overall chopping operation being carefully cut so that proper curvature is maintained as they are welded together again.

■ Finally a little body filler is used to finish off the welded areas after they have been worked into shape with hammer and dolly.

CHAPTER THREE
1955 Chevrolet four door wagon

EVERY TOP CHOPPING PROJECT IS DIFFERENT. ANYONE who has chopped more than a couple of vehicles is aware of that and as we pointed out in the introductory chapter, the most important part of a good top chop operation is the thinking and calculating part before you start. That thinking and calculating process is most important when you look at chopping later model vehicles where sloping pillars and wraparound windshields come into play.

The subject of this chapter is a little different from the norm in that it is a '55 Chevy four door wagon. While there is no doubt that such a vehicle doesn't normally enjoy prominence in the custom car world, you will realise by the end of this chapter that could very well change. The operation is quite a challenge and one that should probably only be attempted by someone already experienced in top chopping, but there is much that can be learned by even the novice in following along with this article.

After several hours eyeballing and measuring the vehicle in preparation for carrying out the chopping operation it is time to make a start. First and very important part of the operation is to jack the vehicle clear of the floor and mount the chassis on solid stands so that the suspension doesn't have any influence on the car. Use shims where necessary between the chassis and the stands to ensure that the vehicle is sitting level and the first part of the process is complete.

Next we need to ensure that when the top is initially removed from the vehicle the door pillars and cowl section all stay in their positions. This is best done by removing the doors and tailgate and building a substantial frame inside the body that picks up on all the door pillars and the tailgate opening. We were fortunate in this regard in that we still had the main part of the frame used when chopping the top of another vehicle. This was used again as the main part of our frame for the Chevy. Consequently we only had to make up the pillar to pillar sections and the cross braces. The pillar sections have plates at their ends that bolt into place in the upper hinge and door latch locations. Now when the roof comes off everything remaining will stay exactly where it is!

The method used in this top chopping operation is to take a two inch slice out of the door pillar areas of the body plus an additional inch out of the near vertical sides of the turret itself. This will give the chopped roofline a more pleasing profile as the turret is quite high compared to later model vehicles. Once the roof is chopped it would took top heavy if the turret remained stock.

Now it's time to get down to the marking out process. To make this easy I used a small section of two inch wide steel plate and worked from pillar to pillar marking out the two inch section to be removed according to predetermined positions from our pre-chop calculations. At the front of the wagon this corresponded roughly to the center of the pillars, but at the rear the cut needs to be made close to the bottom of the forward slanting pillar for reasons that will become obvious as we progress.

It is important to remember when marking out the pillars that we are taking a two inch section horizontally through the pillars so the marking out section of steel needs to remain horizontal at all times even though the pillar concerned may be sloping.

PART ONE

Before starting any cutting the turret section is also marked out using our two inch steel template and a one inch piece to mark out a one inch section for later removal along the side of the turret. This marking out process proceeded right around the roof using the bottom of the rain gutter as our base reference point (see photos for clarification).

It still isn't time to start cutting as there is more measuring and checking to do yet. Remember the smart top chopper's adage, measure twice, cut once!

The side pillars of the wagon slant inward toward the top which means that as the top comes down the roof needs to spread about 7/16" for the pillars to match up again. Normally that would mean that on a roof like this a split would have to be made right down the length of the panel and a section added in to make up the difference. One alternative is to obtain a second roof and cut them both slightly over center and you end up with only one weld right down the center. This was the method we used on the early Falcon sedan delivery chop shown elsewhere in this book. Obtaining a second roof for a '55 Chev wagon in

■ This "before" shot from the rear of the wagon shows the high profile of the turret and the sloping rear pillars that will require some careful measuring and cutting to keep the alignment correct.

■ From the near front on view the slant of the door pillars becomes evident as does the shape of the upper sections of the windshield pillars. Again careful calculations will be required here.

Australia isn't an easy task and after careful consideration I came up with what I think is a better solution that will make the end result more pleasing and require less difficult welding.

The method we will use here is to remove the entire turret skin in one piece where marked at the lower point on the sides for our one inch sectioning. Before doing this though a series of support bows were made up to match the curvature of the underside of the roof so that they will support it in its correct position when the turret goes back on. These were clamped to the inner body support frame initially so that they can be removed and then later put back in position three inches lower than they were. This will position the turret correctly, allowing for the two inch pillar chop and the one inch turret sectioning.

The two stock under roof support bows can now be removed, (they are only spot welded in place) and at last it is time to start cutting. The stock bows will be modified and refitted once the chop is finished.

As mentioned earlier the initial cut is made at the lower marking on the side of the turret so that we can remove the entire roof panel in one piece. The one inch side section isn't removed at this stage for reasons that again will become evident later in the process. A hand grinder fitted with a cut off wheel was used to cut along the lower scribed line leaving a short section uncut in several places around the roof so that it doesn't wobble around too much as we go.

At the windshield end the roof panel is cut straight across some eight or nine inches back from the top of the opening so that the cut is clear of the upper windshield support panel. This will make access much easier when welding the roof back into place as the support panel is fairly close to the underside of the skin at this point. With the skin removed in one piece and set aside we are now left with basically a roof rail joined to the rest of the body by the pillars only. All of a sudden this part of the top chopping operation doesn't look nearly so complicated.

The first cut on the pillars is made at the upper line and again to retain stability in the structure while cutting it, a couple of the pillars on each side are not cut all the way through until last thing. Once they are all cut the roof rail and upper sections of the pillars can be lifted off in one piece and also put aside. Now the two inch section can be cut off the remainder of the pillars.

Sitting the roof rail structure back in place on the body now reveals how well the pieces are going to line up again. Even though the inward taper of the pillars means the tops and bottoms don't line up now, you will be able to see how close the side to side alignment is going to be. Actually pulling the rail structure to one side does allow the pillars to line up almost perfectly. So far, so good.

The center door pillar on these Chevys is quite substantial and actually has an extra reinforcing section running up the middle. Just welding the top and bottom of the pillars back together would mean we don't have access to this center reinforcing section for rewelding. To overcome this problem a short section of the outside skin of the pillar is carefully cut away. Once the center section of the pillar is welded up the outer skin can be welded back in to make the pillar complete again and just as strong as it was originally. Later in this chapter you will see how we further reinforced the pillars but for now we will continue on with the rest of the process.

With the roof rail section sitting in place on the body again we can see how the new lower profile of the roof will change the overall profile of the vehicle. Study the photos and you will see that the front three pillars on each side line up very well with their lower sections but the whole rail section will need to be split and widened in the middle at the front and rear to allow for the spread of the pillars as they come down. The same will have to happen in the rail section above each rear quarter to allow the rear pillars to come back into alignment as well.

■ First step is to mount the chassis rails on stands and shim them until the vehicle is sitting perfectly level with the suspension unloaded. The tires are still touching the floor but not actually holding any of the vehicle's weight.

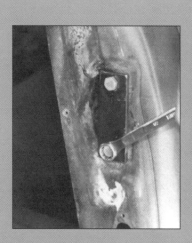
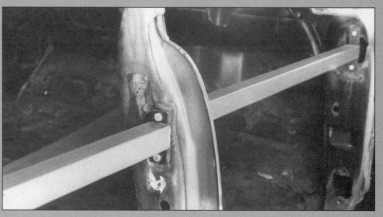

■ Before any cutting is done a substantial frame is built into the body. The door latch mounts and upper hinge mounts are used to bolt the frame into place as are the tailgate latch mounts at the rear. This will ensure that the door pillars and cowl all stay exactly where they are as the chopping operation is carried out.

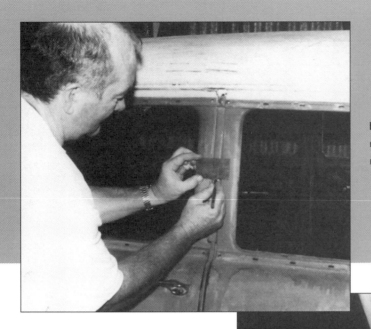

■ A short piece of steel plate is used to mark out the pillars in preparation for removal of a two-inch section.

■ Complex areas like this curved and slanted section of the rear pillars require much careful measuring and calculating so that the cut is made at the most advantageous point to facilitate joining up again. Several different options were marked out before we settled on the most suitable.

■ Having figured out where the best position was for cutting the rear pillars our piece of steel plate came into play again for marking out the two-inch section. Note that the template is always kept horizontal when marking out so that the slant of the pillar doesn't give us a false measurement. This also means all rejoining welds will be horizontal and will make it easier to align the mating pieces.

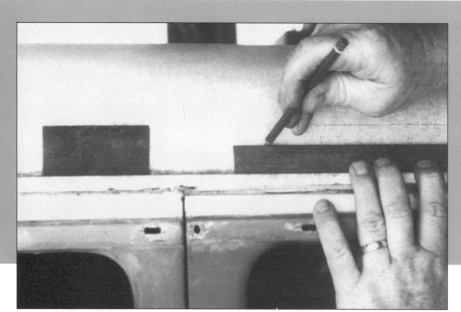

■ A one-inch section of the turret will be removed to give us an overall roof lowering of three-inches. Again pieces of steel strap are used as marking out templates and the bottom of the drip rail used as the base reference point.

■ This photo illustrates how much inward slant there is in the pillars. After cutting, the top section of the pillars will need to be moved outwards by 3/8-inch on each side of the car. Normally that would mean the entire roof skin would need to be split and widened from front to rear; a difficult job. We are going about the process in a different manner on this vehicle.

■ Several bows like this one were made up to duplicate the curvature of the turret and clamped to the reinforcing structure. The stock bows have been removed in preparation for cutting the entire roof skin off in one piece. Later our made up bows will be secured to the reinforcing frame three-inches lower where they will relocate the roof skin in its new position.

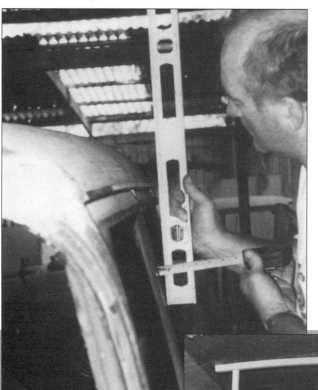

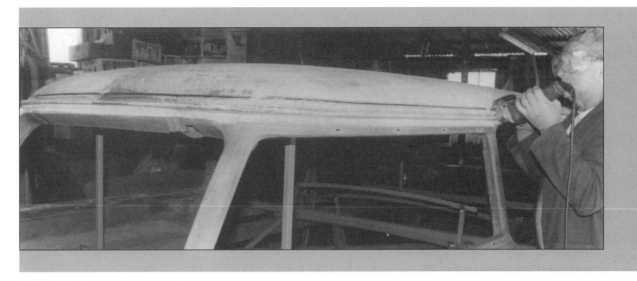

■ Now it is time to start cutting. A cut off wheel in a hand grinder was used to make the first cut at the lower mark on the side of the turret. Note that short sections have been left uncut so that the roof retains some stability while cutting all the way around.

■ Taking the roof skin off leaves us with just a roof rail section joining the tops of all the pillars. At the front the cut across the roof was made about eight-inches back from the windshield opening so that it was clear of the front support rail. This will make later access and welding much easier.

■ Time to cut the pillars. The first cuts are made at the upper marking and again some pillars weren't initially cut all the way through so that some stability is retained while the operation proceeds.

■ Once all the pillars are cut, the roof rail section can be removed in one piece and set aside.

■ Before fitting the roof rail section back on the body all the joining surfaces are cleaned up with a grinder to leave a nice even surface for welding.

■ Now the two-inch sections can be removed from the pillars to give us the required height reduction.

■ The center door pillar has an inner reinforcing section that can't be welded if we just join the pillars back together. The answer is to remove a short section of the outer skin as shown here to provide access to the inner panel for welding. The short section will be welded back in place later.

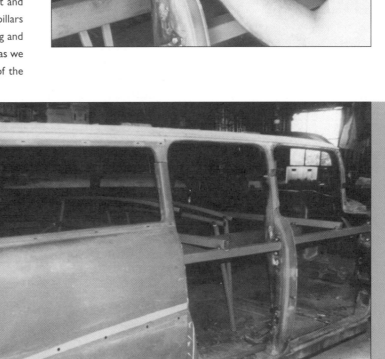

■ Pulling the roof rail section to one side shows that the door pillars will line up very well. However the front and back sections of the rail will need to be split to allow the roof to spread to compensate for the sloping pillars so that they line up again on both sides of the vehicle. The rear quarter rails will also need to be cut and lengthened so that the rear sloping pillars will line up again. The intricate cutting and filling operations will be shown later as we get into the time consuming parts of the top chopping operation.

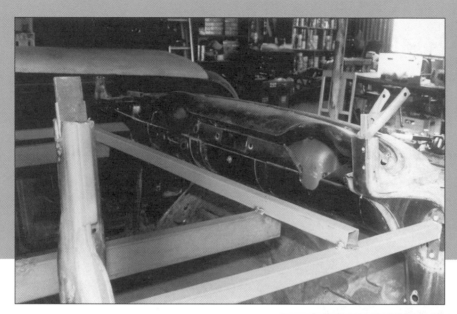

■ Heavy steel plates were made up to be inserted in the center door pillars to act as reinforcements and to provide an upper seat belt mount. Note how they have extensions near the middle to allow them to lock into a slot cut into the pillar so that they are totally captured within the pillar when welded in place.

■ Short sections of box steel tube were used to make reinforcements for the windshield and rear door pillars. Welding them in place will ensure the pillars are stronger than original. Note how the original pillars have also been drilled to allow for extra plug welds above and below the join.

■ With the pillar reinforcements in place in the lower half of the pillars on one side the roof rail can be dropped in place on this side for perfect alignment.

Getting everything back in alignment and adding strength to the pillars

IN PART ONE THE BASIC CHOP WAS COMPLETED AND the roof rail section placed back in position on the pillars. To allow the pillars to line up on both sides of the vehicle the top of the windshield opening and the top of the rear section of the roof rail need to be split. This will allow each half of the roof to move outward as it comes down and consequently all the forward pillars will now line up again. However before making this cut there are several other parts of the operation that need to be completed to keep everything in alignment.

Before we start welding the pillars back into position, we need to take the opportunity to add some extra strength into them and at the same time provide for future fittings such as seat belt mounts. The original center pillar is by far the strongest of the original pillars as it has an extra internal pillar that adds greatly to its strength. This was the one we showed earlier, where we had to cut away an extra section of the outer skin to allow access to the inner pillar for complete welding.

In the same area of this inner pillar is where an upper seat belt mount would logically be located so we need to ensure that it is strong enough for that purpose. To accomplish this, slots were cut vertically into the upper and lower sections of the pillar and sections of the inner pillar cut out completely for a few inches above and below where the join in the pillar will be. A heavy plate insert was then cut to shape so that it has an extension on each side at its mid-point and so that the overall plate itself corresponds in size and shape to the opening in the inner pillars. The extensions are there to fit into the slots we cut into the pillars so that the plate will essentially be locked into the pillar right through the area where all the welding will take place. This is probably better understood by studying the photos. The extensions and slot arrangement also gives us a much larger area for welding and for spreading the load into the pillar in the event of and accident.

The windshield and rear door pillars also need extra reinforcement as they are welded back together to ensure they are stronger than they were originally This was accomplished by inserting short lengths of box tube steel into each pillar at the join. Rather than just rely on the weld joining the pillars together to also retain the reinforcing tube we drilled several holes above and below the join area so plug welds could be used to hold the inserts in several places. Initially, these reinforcing sections were welded into the lower halves of the pillars on one side of the car only. Next the complete roof rail was moved to this side and dropped over the inserts in the pillars. Because all our cuts have

been horizontal this leaves the pillars on the other side still sitting on each other, they just don't align to the outside edges any more.

Now it is time to tack weld the pillars that are aligned. Before cutting the center of the windshield and rear of the roof rail and moving them over so that the opposite side pillars align, simple supports were welded slightly off center in the openings So that they will stay in place once the other side is cut free. Later we will have to weld in filler sections at this point and these supports will ensure the openings maintain their shape accurately. With the supports in place the center cuts were made releasing the opposite side of the roof rail.

The pillar reinforcement/ alignment inserts can now be welded into the lower sections of the pillars on this side as well and this side of the roof dropped into place. Before we can tack weld the roof rail into place, on this side of the wagon, we need to make and fit reinforcing inserts for the upper windshield rail and the upper tailgate-opening rail in similar fashion to the ones used in the side pillars. Once again short sections of box steel tube were used to make these inserts and again the photos better illustrate how they were made than words

PART TWO

can explain. These upper reinforcing sections were slipped into place before G-clamps and short sections of steel strap were used to realign the front and rear openings. Now the side pillars can be tack welded on this side and the upper reinforcements tack welded as well This makes the roof rail essentially one piece again and we can see that it is all going to plan so far.

At this stage, everything from the rear door pillars forward is back in alignment. The outer pillars that don't line up as original again are the very rear ones either side of the tailgate. To overcome this the rear section of the roof rail needs to be cut free at some point in the top of the rear quarter windows. This allows the rear section to be moved back until the pillars line up again but of course this opens up a gap in the roof rail that needs to be filled. Sections of sheet metal could be used to fill this gap but we also need a short length of drip rail. Fortunately we were able to obtain some short sections of wagon roof from a fellow Chevy enthusiast which enabled us to simply cut out the required filler piece, complete with drip rail attached. This made filling the rail back in again very easy and the end result is neat and tidy. The photos show how little extra work was needed at the base of the rear pillars to make their shape conform to the original again.

Once all the pillars were tack welded into place and the rear pillars finished, we could go back and fully weld all the other pillars and the center sections of the windshield opening and rear tailgate opening. After welding up the pillars we finished off the roof rail extensions as well.

This wagon originally came with a two-piece tailgate but owner Lyle Simpson prefers the one-piece style. The one piece unit swings from the top of the opening in similar fashion to the original upper tailgate but the hinges are physically larger. That means the hinge mounts that are formed into the upper inner panel need to be replaced and there is no better time to do that than now, while the roof skin is still off the vehicle.

New hinge mounts were made up from short lengths of angle iron that were drilled to accept the hinges before being fitted into the vehicle. Next the original hinge mounts were carefully cut away after marking where the new ones will need to locate in the upper panel. A MIG welder was then used to tack weld the new hinge mounts into place with a length of box tube used to clamp across the two hinge mounts to ensure they were aligned with each other.

Since we still have our inner body frame in place we can't actually fit the entire tailgate in its closed position. However we need to shorten and widen the glass area to suit the chopped top. The top of the tailgate was cut off through the glass area and the two-inch section removed from the remaining pillars. The top rail of the tailgate was then cut through the middle and widened by welding in a filler strip. This was done with the pillars tack welded back into place to maintain alignment. Once the top section was fully welded the tack welds on the pillars were removed again to allow us to use just the top section for fitting up to the hinges in the body. Later when we remove the frame from inside the body, we can weld the lower section of the tailgate back into place and finalize its alignment all around. This completes the difficult part of the roof chop. All that remains is to refit the turret and chop the doors. Sounds easy! !

■ We need to cut the center of the windshield and rear of the roof rail to allow the opposite side to move over to its new location but before we do, the openings have supports tack welded into them just slightly off center. Now when we cut the roof rail in half lengthwise, we have a stable reference point to work back to.

■ Steel strap and G-clamps are used to align the top of the windshield opening while the gap in between is reinforced and filled.

■ Odd sections and combinations of box steel tube were used to make the reinforcements for the windshield rail and the upper rear rail. The windshield rail had an unusually shaped original reinforcing piece inside it at this point. To make the new reinforcement easier to fit the lower section of the rail was cut away as shown in the photo. This took out the original reinforcement that was attached to the lower part of the rail only and allowed us to fit an entire custom made box tube section inside the rail. The method of cutting out the original piece also gives a greater welding area for the new reinforcement. This area is now very strong.

■ To reinforce the rear rail, four pieces of box steel tube were found to be exactly right to fill the area when slightly offset to each other as shown in the photo. These four pieces were then slipped into the rail and manipulated into place as the rail was fitted back in place. Now all that remains is to weld them permanently into position.

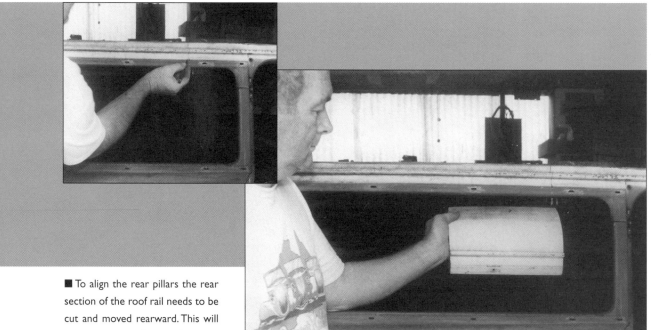

■ To align the rear pillars the rear section of the roof rail needs to be cut and moved rearward. This will open up a gap that needs to be filled. In this case we were fortunate to be able to obtain a short section of spare roof from another wagon enabling us to cut out a filler piece that even includes a section of the original drip rail.

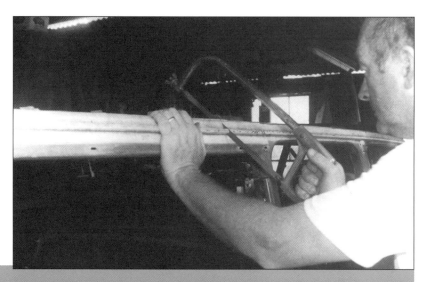

■ Now the rear section of the roof rail can be cut free again and moved rearwards and the filler piece welded into place.

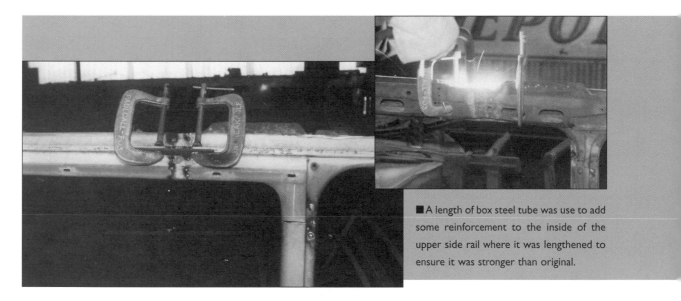

■ A length of box steel tube was use to add some reinforcement to the inside of the upper side rail where it was lengthened to ensure it was stronger than original.

■ The only extra work needed at this end was to add a small rounded section at the base to duplicate the original shape of the window opening.

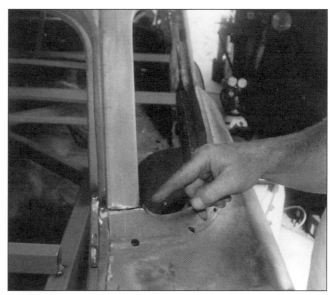

■ Finally all the pillars were fully welded and the cover piece, removed earlier from the center pillar, welded back into place to make the basic roof rail section all complete again as shown below. We were able to salvage a small section from the original piece of pillar that was removed in the chopping process to achieve this.

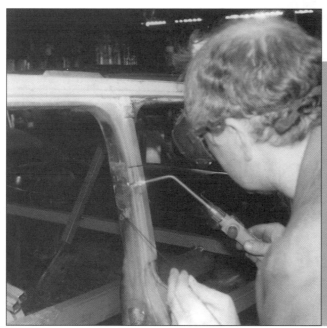

■ The pillars have heavy sections of metal inside them and thinner sheet metal skins on the outside. A MIG or wire feed welder was used to weld the heavier sections back together.

■ The outer sheet metal sections are welded together using the oxy-acetylene torch, leaving a softer weld bead that can be cleaned up easily. A small section of metal was added into the lower inside edge of the quarter panel window opening to make the curve complete again.

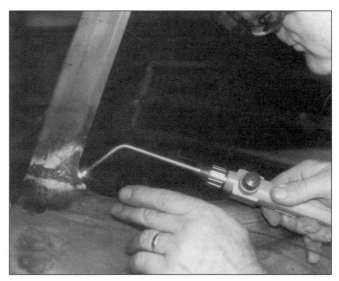

■ This completes the basic chopping operation with regard to the pilar sections and now we can turn our attention to the roof skin once more.

■ After cutting out the original hinge mounts new ones were made from angle iron. A length of box steel tube was used to align the hinges while they were tack welded into place.

■ The upper section of the tailgate was chopped and widened first, then removed from the tailgate proper to allow for hinge alignment. The entire tailgate won't be able to be refitted until later, when the inner body frame is removed from the vehicle.

■ Having removed the top section of the widened upper tailgate we can now use it to check and adjust the alignment of the hinge mounts before permanently welding them in place.

■ This photo shows the hinge itself bolted into position on the new mount. Having the roof skin removed makes this much easier to achieve.

■ Now that the hinge mounts are completed the locating brace for the upper roof rail can be removed and we are ready to start the final part of the chopping operation. All that is left is to refit the turret and chop the doors.

Altering the profile of the roof skin and welding it back in place.

WITH ALL THE CHOPPING OF THE PILLARS AND THE extension work done to the roof rail and upper windshield opening completed, it is now time to look at making the roof of the '55 wagon complete. If you have followed along with this exercise since the beginning, you will remember that we took the entire roof skin off in one piece. At that stage it was our intention to remove about a one-inch section from the sides of the roof skin to lower its profile. This wasn't done straight away as I had a feeling we may not need to take that much out in the end.

Now that the rail section is all complete again, we can sit the skin back on and assess what needs to be done next. Because the side pillars of the vehicle are slanted the roof skin needs to "grow" as it comes down for the edges to meet again. Sitting the skin back in place indicated that this "growth" needed to be somewhere in the order of 1-1/2 inches overall, or about 3/4 of an inch each side. My original scheme was to spread the edges of the roof skin and lean the short sections that remain on the roof rail inward until the edges met again. This would have the effect of lowering the overall height of the roof skin and overcome the need to split and widen the roof right down the center, an exercise that involves lots of difficult welding and subsequent beating and stretching to maintain the shape of the roof.

Sitting the roof skin in place on top of the roof rail allowed me to eyeball the best way to proceed with the refitting of the panel to the roof rail. With the skin sitting in place, it was evident that the curve of the sides is not consistent from front to rear. The further towards the rear you go the more upright the sides of the roof skin become. The stock roof also has a visible hump towards the rear in the center of the panel. It isn't noticed on the stock vehicle but now that our pillars are shorter the roof would look top heavy if left this way. My continued "eyeballing" suggested that the roof skin needed to be trimmed more at the rear than at the front to keep everything in proportion.

Starting from the front a line was drawn from the very tip of the leading edge of the side of the roof skin all the way to the rear where the line ended up approximately 3/4 inch above the edge. In other words a tapered section of the edge of the roof skin would be removed varying from nothing at the front edge to 3/4 inch wide at and across the rear. Taking out a section of this shape achieved two things. First it compensates for the fact that there is less material to stretch outward at the front end of the roof because it is less upright at this end. Secondly, the

removal of the wider section towards the rear allows us to take out the hump effect in the middle of the rear section of the roof as the sides are stretched outward.

Next the short section of roof skin that remains attached to the roof rails was carefully and slowly hammered inward all around the edge a little at a time working all around the roof rail. This exercise reduced the gap between this short upright section and the recently trimmed roof skin by about one third. Small vertical cuts were made at the rear corners to allow the radius of these corner sections to be reduced as the hammering took place. Now we need to stretch the edges of the skin outward to meet this point where we will be able to weld them back together again. How to achieve this stretching operation was the subject of considerable thought before actually embarking on the process. Before the stretching could be undertaken more vertical cuts were made in the roof skin at the rear corners to allow them to open up slightly as the edge was stretched outward.

Essentially, this is how the stretching was achieved. Two pieces of 3x2-inch lumber were clamped to each side of the edge of the roof skin as shown in the photos. A single large G-clamp was used for this. Next the G-clamp was gripped firmly and rotated so that it gently bent the edge of the roof skin outward and slightly flattened the panel at the same time. In next to no time at all the two edges were meeting again.

At the very rear of the roof it was now evident that more of the skin needed to be removed to allow the edges to meet evenly all the way around the entire roof panel. Slowly and carefully, this rear section was marked and trimmed until it all met as closely as was possible. With the now stretched roof skin sitting in place its new profile becomes evident and it is very pleasing to the eye. The roof is going to look more in proportion with the side pillars because it is lower and flatter than the

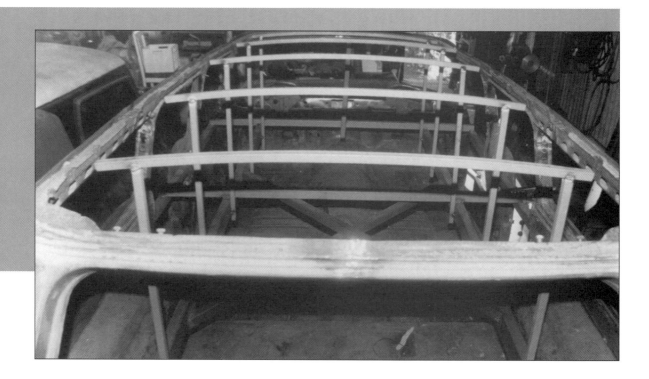

■ Prior to sliding our turret section back onto the roof rails the support bows we made up earlier were refitted to the vehicle in their new position, three inches lower than originally was the case.

■ The wagon finally has its roof back in place as one piece again. This time we show you how the roof skin was stretched and flattened to keep it proportional to the lower profile overall.

original. All we have to do is weld it back in place. For this type of work I prefer to use the oxy acetylene torch as it leaves the welded area softer and more workable than the harder deposit of a MIG welder. Again, great care is needed when carrying out this type of welding on such a large panel as you don't want any excess distortion.

Starting at the rear, the roof tack welds were made where the panels met closest, near the middle and worked outward towards the sides. Short sections were tacked (about three or four inches at a time) and then gently worked with hammer and dolly to keep the panels aligned as work progressed. Once the rear was attached fairly well right across the body the tack welding moved to the front corners on each side, to ensure they stayed in position while we progressed along both sides. Once the front corners were secured, the tack welding was carried out from the rear towards the front again. All the while the hammer and dolly was used to keep everything in alignment as welding progressed. The result was a roof panel completely tack welded in place with no undue distortion evident anywhere.

With the roof skin attached to the body again it is evident that we will finish up with a gap about two inches wide to be filled between the leading edge of the roof and the windshield section. Because we have reduced the profile of the main part of the roof, this windshield section now appears too high in relation to the rest of the roof, but don't panic yet. If you inspect the forward section of the roof above the windshield on a sedan or wagon you will see that it has a much higher profile than say a Sport Coupe or Nomad. I reckoned that we could rework this front section on the wagon to more closely resemble the lower profile of the Coupe or Nomad without removing it from the vehicle. More on this later.

Meanwhile it's back to the welding on the main section of roof. Again starting in the middle at the rear the tack welded join was now fully finish welded. This was carried out in short sections at a time and worked gently with hammer and dolly as work progressed.

Since the weld is close to the edge of the roof, there was little distortion due to the reinforcing nature of the roof rail. Just a little constant attention with the hammer and dolly was all that was required to keep it all in alignment. The vertical expansion and contraction cuts at each rear corner that were mentioned earlier were welded up at the same time as the surrounding joins. By the time the entire roof skin was welded back in place our roof was looking good again. All that remains to be done to this section now is to properly dress the welded area with slapping iron and dolly and clean up the welds with a body grinder.

Where the edge was stretched outward via our clamp and wood method there is a noticeable, slight crease in the panel that needs to be worked out to make the entire outer edge of the roof all the one gently curving plane again. To achieve this the slapping iron and dolly was all that was required. Working along

the roof from front to rear the dolly was held right on the inside of this subtle inward crease and the slapping iron used initially just either side of the crease line. This has the effect of bringing the lowest point of the crease up to the same level as the metal either side of it, (known in panel beating talk as the dolly off method). Once the worked area is basically all back at the same level the slapping iron and dolly are then worked directly onto one another to completely remove any slight high and low spots. The end result is a nicely curved roof edge that, but for the weld line, might have come from the factory that way.

Now we can turn our attention to the front of the roof once more. To achieve the lower profile "Coupe style" roof line above the windshield this eight or nine inch section of roof needs to be pulled down towards its rear edge. To allow this to happen, a hacksaw and the cutting off wheel was used make a curved cut from the rear outer edge around to the front outer corner of the windshield opening. This allows the panel to be pulled down without the corner section putting it under tension. Before we could progress much further on this section though our forward most support brace inside the car had to be removed as it is very close to the front edge of the main roof panel. With it out of the way we can get at the whole area from below much easier.

At this stage it was evident that the front section of the main roof panel was under fairly severe tension. When we tried to lift it up to somewhere near where it will need to finish up it caused the roof skin to buckle just behind the front edge. To overcome this tendency a cut was made from the center back into the roof panel for about ten inches. This relieved the tension but didn't totally overcome the tendency to buckle when lifted. Our front support brace that was removed was reinstalled at the point where this cut ended in the panel to keep it supported while we fill in the gap. This support brace prevented the panel from buckling as we lifted and welded pieces into the gap.

We still have a gap in the center of the front section of roof panel where the windshield opening was widened to make up for the taper of the pillars on each side. A short section of sheet metal was used to fill this in again at this point. Now the entire forward section can be pulled down closer to alignment with the main part of the roof. By now it was evident that some stretching will be needed in this area as it is all joined together and filled in again, but it isn't so severe that we can't cope with it by taking our time and working it all into position as we go. Initially a small square of sheet metal was clamped into the center of the roof to temporarily bring the front and rear sections together. Now the rest of the front section can be pulled down into position at the outer edges. This action immediately shows that a tapered section needs to be trimmed off each end before the curved cut to the windshield can be welded up to retain the outer edges of this forward section in their new lower position.

Now all that is left is to fill in the gap between the forward and rear sections with sheet metal to make the roof absolutely complete again. To do this, short sections were cut to shape and welded into the gap from the outer edges inward. Using pieces up to about nine inches long in each stage allows the filler panel and its surrounding area to be stretched upward as we go to bring all this forward section of roof back into the one gently curving plane.

Stretching was achieved by bumping up the area with a large ball peen hammer and dressing it off with hammer or slapping iron and dolly as required. Working from side to side, in these short sections allows you to gauge your progress and make corrections as you go. This is time consuming work but the end result is well worth the effort.

With all the roof back as one piece again, the final operation for this part of the project is to clean up all the welds with a body grinder and work the panel to remove any remaining high and low spots. This brings us to the final part of the top chop operation overall, the chopping and refitting of the doors and tailgate. Now that the roof is complete the reinforcing frame can be removed from inside the vehicle and the doors chopped to complete the project.

■ First step in refitting the roof skin was to sit it back in place on top of the roof rail. This allows us to gauge how much it will need to stretch to meet up with the short original section remaining around the edge of the rail. Look at the outer edges and you can see the difference.

■ To reduce the gap between the roof skin and the short upright section of skin left on the roof rail this short section will be bent inwards slightly. To allow this to happen without buckling around the rear corners three vertical cuts were made with the hacksaw at each corner.

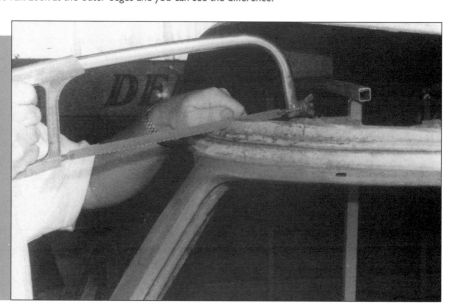

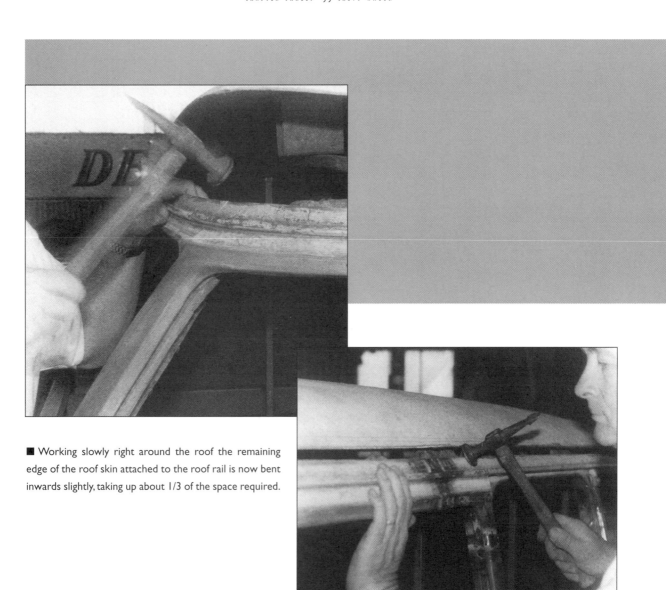

■ Working slowly right around the roof the remaining edge of the roof skin attached to the roof rail is now bent inwards slightly, taking up about 1/3 of the space required.

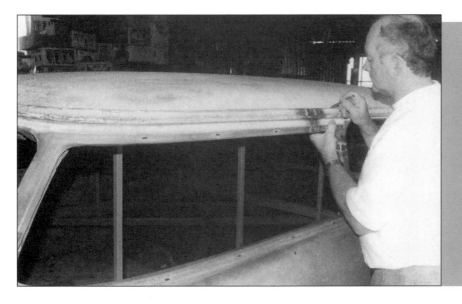

■ To maintain an even profile to the roof overall, we calculated that the skin could be reduced in height by removing a tapered section from front to rear right around the edge. The piece removed varied from nothing right at the front to 3/4 of an inch at the rear corners. See the text for full details on this operation.

■ Despite removing the 3/4 inch section towards and around the rear of the roof skin, we found an extra piece needed to come off right across the very rear section of the roof skin. This was necessary to leave us with an even gap right around the roof skin ready for stretching to meet up with the remaining piece on the roof rail.

■ The hand grinder was used to clean up all the mating edges to get them fitting as neatly as possible. The better the fit the easier the welding process is and the less work is involved in keeping warpage to a minimum.

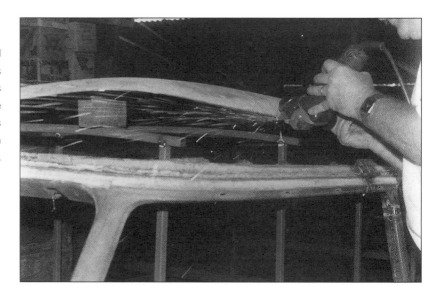

■ As with the short section on the roof rail several cuts were made in the rear corner of the roof skin to allow it to open outwards as the sides and rear were stretched. These cuts extend into the skin about three inches in each case.

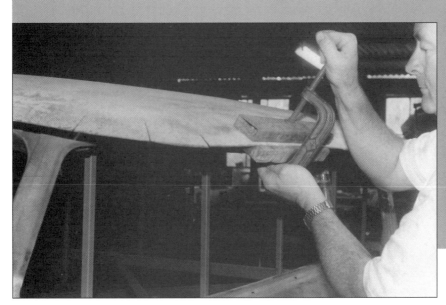

■ To flatten the edges and move them outwards two pieces of wood were clamped either side of the panel and retained with a large G-clamp. To achieve the outward "stretch" the G-clamp was simply grasped and rotated upwards, working right around the roof skin.

■ Now the stretched roof skin sits back in place in the roof rail ready for welding back in place. Note how the profile of the roof overall is now more pleasing and more in proportion with the overall lower profile of the vehicle.

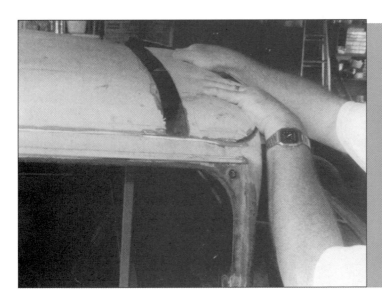

■ Now we can also roughly align the remaining front section of the roof as well before we start welding. The front corners were cut around to the top of the windshield opening as shown to allow this piece of the roof panel to lay down more. The end result will be a front of roof profile that more closely matches that of a Sports Coupe rather than a sedan or wagon.

■ Finally our roof skin is ready to be tack welded back in place. This we commenced in the middle at the rear with tack welds placed 3/4 inch apart.

■ This is a very large panel and we don't want it moving around too much while welding so once the rear was tack welded we moved to the front and tacked the front corners in place.

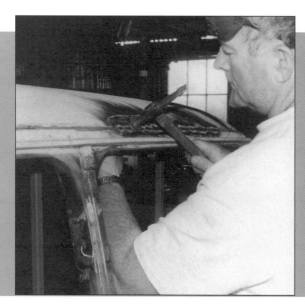

■ Hammer and dolly were used with restraint to keep the panels in alignment as tack welding progressed. Don't overdo the hammer and dolly work at this stage as we don't want to 'work harden' the area too much.

■ Once the tack welding is completed, we can stand back and survey our handiwork. Note how the overall profile now looks as it should. The finished vehicle won't look top heavy as it would if the turret retained its original profile.

■ Final welding can now take place again working from rear to front and with gentle hammer and dolly work as we go, just enough to keep it all in alignment. Short sections (about two-three inches) were welded at a time and then worked lightly with hammer and dolly.

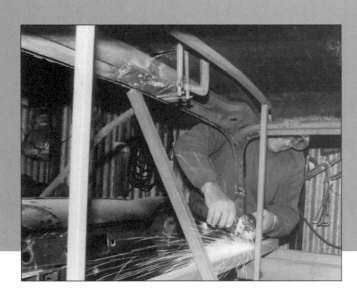

■ Now we can turn our attention to the front of the roof. A filler panel will need to be added to make up the gap between the main roof skin and the forward section. This gap is right alongside our forward inner roof support so it must be removed.

■ For the front section to lay down in profile and be welded at the corners again a tapered piece needs to be cut from the outer corners as shown.

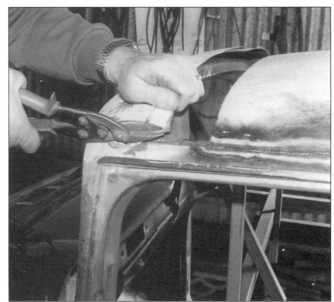

■ With the outer corners rewelded again we can pull the rest of the panel down into position. It is already evident that the center of this forward section is going to tend to pull down too tightly. It will need stretching to keep the roof shape all in proportion.

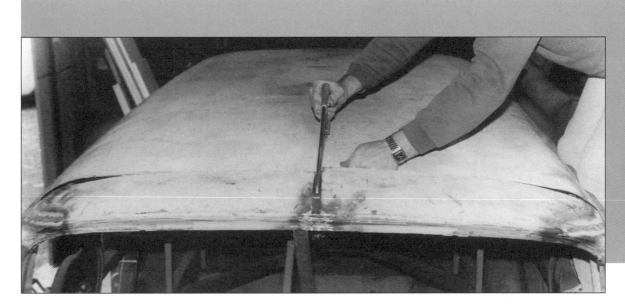

■ To allow for some tension to be taken out of the forward section of the roof skin a cut was made back into the main panel for about nine inches.

■ The gap in the center of the forward panel has now been filled in with sheetmetal. G-clamps and a square piece of metal was now used to clamp the front section and the main roof panel together at this point. Now we can see that the two sections will match up fairly well.

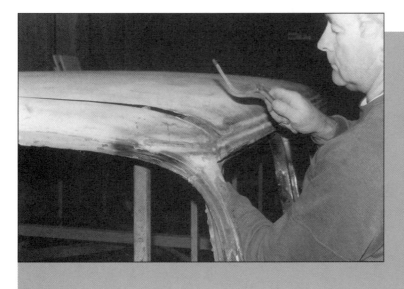

■ Rather than try to weld in a one-piece filler strip we elected to fill the forward gap a little at a time. This will allow us to work each piece into shape as we go.

■ Right from the start it was evident that we would have to stretch this area upwards as we go. Here a large hammer is being used to bump up the first filled section before moving on.

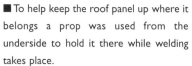

■ To help keep the roof panel up where it belongs a prop was used from the underside to hold it there while welding takes place.

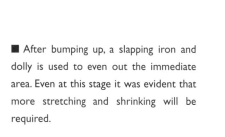

■ After bumping up, a slapping iron and dolly is used to even out the immediate area. Even at this stage it was evident that more stretching and shrinking will be required.

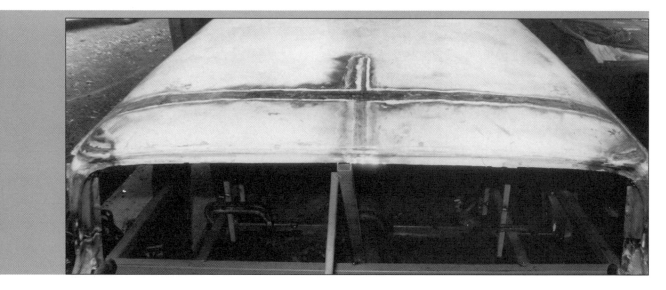

Finishing the roof skin and chopping the tops of the doors

FINALLY THE TOP CHOPPING OPERATION ON THE '55 Chevy wagon is complete! When we left you the entire lowering of the roof itself was completed, essentially leaving only the chopping of the doors, refitting of the one piece tailgate and minor cleaning up to be done. Here's how the last stages of the operation were carried out.

First, let's backtrack just a little to show you how one minor finishing touch was performed on the roof skin. When we used our clamp and wood method to stretch the outer edge of the roof skin outwards it did leave a minor kink right along the panel. Now that the entire roof skin is welded in position we were able to go back with slapping iron and dolly and work this kink out, giving the edges of the roof its nice rounded shape again. All that was then needed was to clean up the welded areas with a body disc in a nine-inch sander.

Earlier, we mentioned several times how the forward section of the roof wanted to pull down as we filled it. By filling it in sections we managed to keep this shrinking to a minimum, but still it was obvious that we would need to stretch the area when finished and work it back into shape with the rest of the roof. Only one way to do this and that is to lay right into it with a heavy hammer and bump the area up where it is pulling down too tightly and then use a series of shrinks and work with slapping iron and dolly to even out the area again. The photos show that this was no small task but the end result was a roof that conforms to shape all the way to the front. More work will be required on this area before paint time but for now it is back in shape and we can move onto the doors.

Before we can tackle the doors it is finally time for us to remove the inner framework that held the whole body together while the top was chopped. This frame is the secret to keeping everything in alignment while doing a top chop. Don't try chopping a car without fitting such a brace.

The hand grinder came into play to first remove all the remaining roof support bows followed by the cross braces and finally the main frame. At this stage the support brace that had been holding the center of the windshield opening in place was also removed to leave our body as a completely bare shell again. To chop the doors they were first fitted to the body again, one at a time and marked out for the removal of the two-inch section through the pillars. This is quite straightforward and simple as the tops of the doors are symmetrical and uniform in thickness of the pillars. The front doors were chopped first followed by the rears. Just one minor hiccup on the rear doors

was encountered. When first marked out for removal of the two inch section we found that the forward pillar area if shortened where we marked it would have taken out an anti-rattle rubber bump stop. In order to preserve this feature of the door we simply re-marked the forward pillar lower down so that the rubber bumper was left in position.

With all four doors chopped and closed the wagon now looks like a complete vehicle again. The one piece tailgate was next. This was chopped earlier in the project but not mated back together again as our inner body frame prevented it from being fitted into its opening. Now that the frame is out the two halves can be joined again while being aligned in its opening. The tailgate is like the doors in that it is essentially symmetrical so this is quite a straightforward operation as well.

Only one more thing to do before the wagon can go back to its owner. There were originally two inner roof support bows that were removed early in the top chopping operation. These need to be refitted but they also need to be reshaped to follow the new profile of the roof. For most of their length they are okay but at the outer ends they are now too short. The ends bend downward too abruptly and too far. However all that was needed to make them fit again

PART FOUR

was to rework the ends by carefully "de-radiusing" the bends. This was done by slipping the ends into the open jaws of a vise and bending them outwards, a little at a time, and working around the bend. In no time at all, they were reshaped to suit the lower profile roof and they didn't need to be cut and lengthened. The bows were fitted back into the wagon using large self-tapping screws to allow them to be removed again for fitting of new inner roof insulation material. Once that is done they can be welded into position.

Originally we had intended that we would make a pattern and have a brand new windshield made to suit the wagon. However now that the top chop is completed we have made a surprising

■ After many hours work and lots of careful measuring the top chop on the '55 Chevy wagon is complete. Two inches were removed through the pillars and a further one-inch height reduction was achieved by taking a section out of the sides of the roof turret. The sides of the roof were then recontoured to give us the pleasing and proportional profile evident in this photo.

■ Slapping iron and dolly was used to remove the crease left by the outward stretching of the roof edge as shown earlier in this chapter. The radius of the edge of the roof was left even all the way around as a result.

■ All that was needed to finish up this area was to clean up the welded and worked area with a body disc in a nine-inch sander.

discovery. The original windshield glass was laid back into the opening as best it could be to reveal that the shape hadn't really changed all that much apart from the height difference. With tape measure in hand I went measuring on a Sport Coupe and found that there is very little difference in height between the new opening and a stock Sport Coupe. It appears it will be a simple job to grind a little off the top of a Sport Coupe windshield and it will fit the wagon! What a bonus!

That's it, the top chop is complete. From this point the wagon went back to Canberra where owner Lyle Simpson was busy preparing a fully detailed chassis for it.

This has been one of the most involved top chops I have ever undertaken, due mostly to the sheer size of the roof concerned. Like most top chops the secret to getting them right is lots of deep thought and careful measuring before you start cutting.

■ The forward area of the roof that required filling needed a fair amount of reworking because it had shrunk and pulled down. The only way to correct this is to stretch it back the other way then shrink and beat it until the required contour is achieved. Here a heavy hammer is being used to bump and stretch up the area.

■ Next the high spots are heated with a torch in preparation for shrinking again. Each application of heat should be about the size of your thumbnail and heated until red.

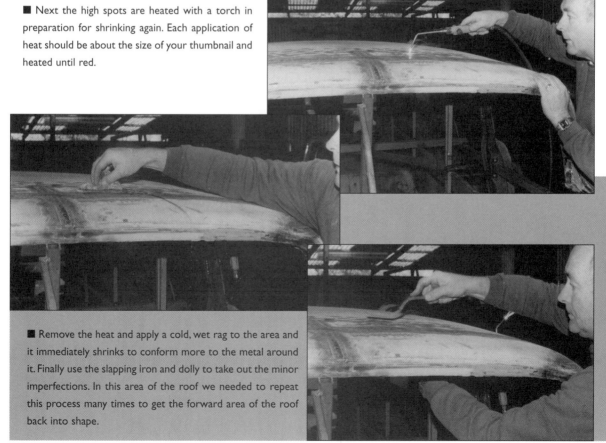

■ Remove the heat and apply a cold, wet rag to the area and it immediately shrinks to conform more to the metal around it. Finally use the slapping iron and dolly to take out the minor imperfections. In this area of the roof we needed to repeat this process many times to get the forward area of the roof back into shape.

■ This photo shows the area that needed bumping up and shrinking as explained on the previous page. As you can see by the number of dark spots quite a few shrinks were needed but we managed to get the roof back into shape and free of any "oil canning".

■ With the roof area completed we could finally remove the supports and the body frame from inside the vehicle. A hand grinder was used to cut the solid tack welds holding it all together. Don't attempt a top chop like this without fitting some form of bracing inside the body so that everything stays in place when the roof comes off.

■ Now we can stand back and appreciate the new overall profile of the vehicle. The doors are next.

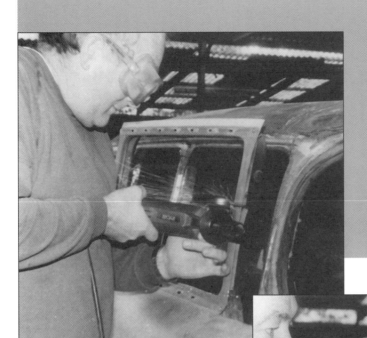

■ Time to fit the doors one at a time and chop them down to size too. They are quite straightforward since the tops of the doors are symmetrical and upright.

■ The two inch section was cut out and the tops placed back into position to make sure they were correct with the door closed.

■ Then they were welded in place to give us a complete door again.

■ A minor hiccup was encountered on the rear doors when we almost cut out the two inch section right where there is a rubber anti-rattle bumper. To retain this feature the cut was simply moved further down the pillar.

■ Below: With all the doors chopped and sitting in position the wagon now takes on a whole new profile when viewed from the side. Proportions are just right and you can now see the benefits of lowering the profile of the turret section. The rear quarter windows are available new in laminated glass and will only need their tops cut down. Rear pillar angle is the same as original.

■ The one-piece tailgate gets the same treatment as the doors and only needed to be welded back together since we had widened the upper section earlier in the project. Now that the inner body support frame has been removed it could be fitted back into its opening.

■ All that is left to do to complete the whole top chop operation is to refit the original roof support bows. These needed some recontouring at the ends so that they conformed to the new profile of the outer edges of the roof but because the turret has been lowered the bows did not need to be cut and widened to make up for the roof "spread".

■ The bows were secured using large self tapping metal screws to allow them to be removed again later for fitting new under-roof insulation material. They will eventually be welded in place.

■ Finally the top chopping operation is complete and the wagon has returned to owner Lyle Simpson. While the top was being chopped Lyle has been preparing a rolling chassis for the project. We look forward to seeing the finished product.

THERE ARE MANY WAYS TO CHOP THE TOP OF ANY given vehicle. No one particular way is necessarily any better than another but there are some considerations that must be accounted for in any top chopping operation. The main one of these will always be the ability to cut or make a new windshield for the vehicle concerned once the roof has been lowered.

Cars that have what might be termed to have "conventional" windshields are usually fairly straightforward. By "conventional" I mean windshields that have relatively straight windshield pillars that basically slope forward at a constant angle until they reach the top of the cowl. However, tackle a vehicle that has a wrap-around style windshield and suddenly it's a whole new ball game. Before you chop a roof like this, you need to think and plan everything very carefully.

When lowering the roof on any wrap-around windshield style body, there are two basic methods that can be used. One is to essentially bring the roof straight down and then extensively grind the edges and top of the windshield until it can be laid back enough to fit into the new opening. Of course you will need a laminated windshield to be able to do this. The "laid-back" method is okay if the chop isn't too severe, but the windshield needs to be altered and trial fitted as the chopping operation is in progress, to be sure that it will fit when the entire operation is completed. Never, never chop a top like this and worry about the windshield later, or you will most likely find it can't be made to fit. Even when this method is used successfully, it is still often difficult to make the windshield fit properly and the more you have to grind the glass, the greater the risk that it will break.

The second method for chopping a wrap-around type windshield is the one used in the example shown in this chapter, a 1956 Chevy pickup owned at the time by Peter Collier. Larry O'Toole and Harry Wright in Castlemaine, carried out this chopping operation and yet the windshield alterations were done in Canberra, some 400 miles away, where Peter lives. That

sounds like a dangerous course of action, but by using the method shown here most of the risk of a non-fitting windshield is removed. The method we used was to leave the lower 2/3 of the windshield opening in its standard configuration and modify the leading edge of the roof so that it conforms to the shape of the windshield at its new, lowered height. This involves a lot more body work than the first method described in this chapter, (believe me), but we think the end result is more pleasing to the eye and it will certainly be a lot easier for the person who has to modify the windshield to fit.

In this particular case we added another dimension to the operation by carrying out the chop in two distinct stages. Stage one was to take 2-1/2 inches out of the top through the glass area. These '56 Chevy pickups have an unusually high turret in their standard form so the second stage of our chopping operation involved removing another one inch from the near vertical edges of the

PART ONE

turret itself. All this is more easily explained in pictures but it is still quite a long involved operation. Follow along as we bring this pickup down below the cloud level.

■ *Opposite Page:*
Peter Collier's '56 Chevy pickup had been tubbed in preparation for an eventual complete rebuild that would also incorporate a chopped top. This was one of the last photos taken of the pickup prior to the chopping operation. It looks too tall anyway!

■ Having stripped the cabin clean of all fittings including the fuel tank, the first step of the chopping operation was to remove the laminated windshield. Even though this windshield won't be reused in the pickup we wanted to keep it intact for reasons that will become obvious later. To achieve that the rubber was carefully cut away from the outside edge only so that we could also reuse it during the chopping operation at a later stage.

■ Harry Wright and Bob Stevens carefully lift the windshield out of its rubber, leaving the cabin in readiness for an attack on its vertical pillars.

■ Once the roof is off the cabin, there is little supporting the rest of the body and it could easily move out of square during the rest of the operation. To overcome this we stabilized the pickup's chassis on jack stands and built a frame of box tubing into the cabin, connecting the upper door hinge area to the door catch mounts with cross braces running from side to side. This frame also acted as a scaffold later in the project as we worked on the top of the roof.

■ Masking tape was used to mark out the sections of the roof to be removed. On this body we reckoned on 2-1/2 inches being the right amount to take out at this point. Note that the top cut will be right at the bottom edge of curve of the rear window. This allows the window shape to remain proportional and also makes it easier to align the separate pieces as the roof comes down.

■ Now a scribe is used to mark the paint using the edge of the masking tape as a guide. It's worth noting at this point how high the turret is above the drip rail. Later on we'll take an inch out of this section as well, making the total chop 3-1/2 inches. Once the scribing is completed the masking tape is removed and the cutting can begin.

■ The entire roof section was removed in one operation by cutting at the top line. Then the 2-1/2 inch sections were cut from the pillars with a hacksaw. It's easier to cut the sections from the stabilized cabin than from the removed roof panel, hence the reason for doing it in this sequence.

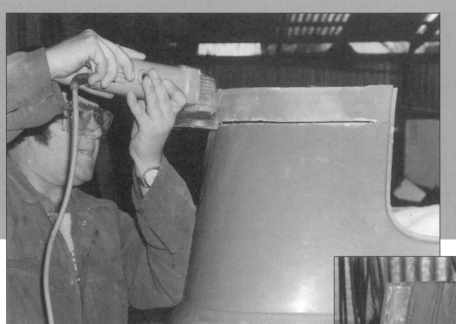

■ The hacksaw was also used to cut through the door pillar area at the rear of the cabin but the rest of this panel was then cut using a cut-off wheel in a hand grinder.

■ Chevy pickups of this era also have an inner metal skin, which will get in the way when it comes time to weld the outer skins back together. For this reason the inner skin was removed from the rear window around to the door pillar as shown here.

■ As the roof comes down it also needs to spread outwards on both sides so that the pieces will align again. Here Harry marks the roof for cutting straight down the middle from front to back.

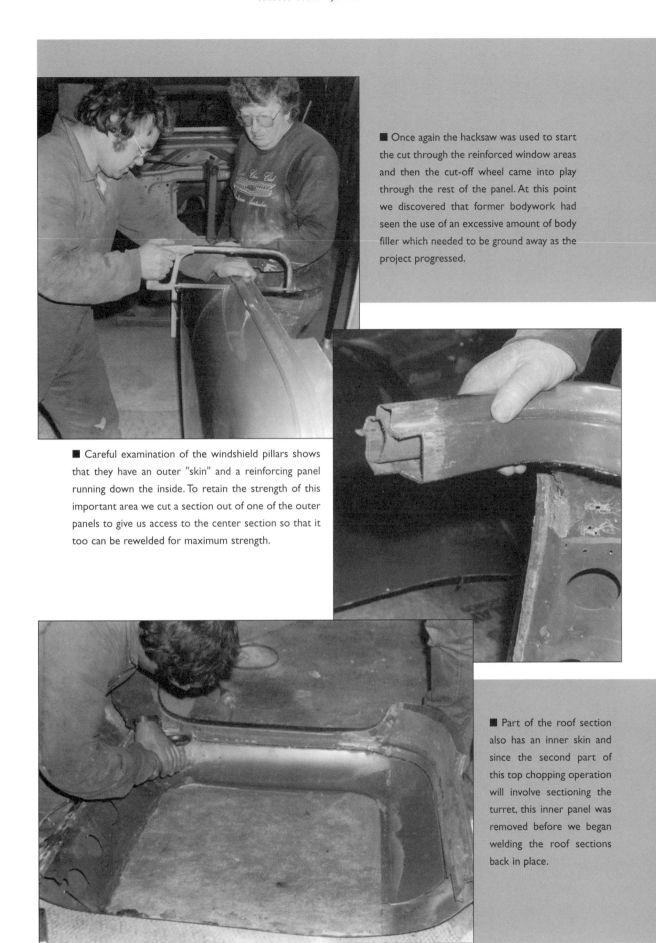

■ Once again the hacksaw was used to start the cut through the reinforced window areas and then the cut-off wheel came into play through the rest of the panel. At this point we discovered that former bodywork had seen the use of an excessive amount of body filler which needed to be ground away as the project progressed.

■ Careful examination of the windshield pillars shows that they have an outer "skin" and a reinforcing panel running down the inside. To retain the strength of this important area we cut a section out of one of the outer panels to give us access to the center section so that it too can be rewelded for maximum strength.

■ Part of the roof section also has an inner skin and since the second part of this top chopping operation will involve sectioning the turret, this inner panel was removed before we began welding the roof sections back in place.

■ Now it's time for a trial fit of one of the roof sections. At this point extra pairs of hands are a bonus. Remember, in our case someone has to take the photos too!

■ With the roof aligned at the door pillar and back of the cabin we can see how much misalignment there is at the windshield pillar. In this case about 1/4 inch, which we will correct by heating and bending the top half of the pillar forward a little bit later in the operation.

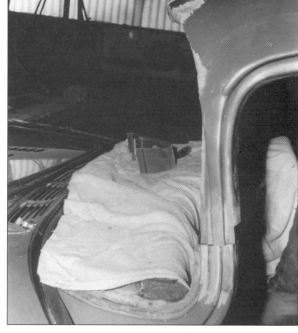

■ With both roof sections now sturdily tacked at the door pillars and rear window we can pay attention to the joins at the center, front and back. These are aligned with a short length of steel strap and clamped into place using vice grips.

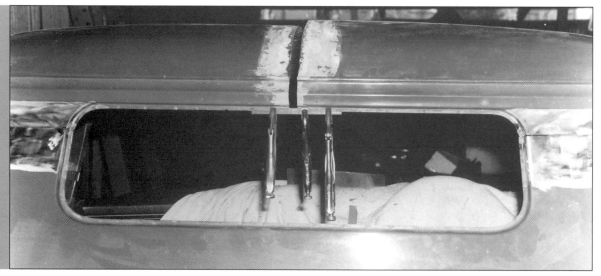

■ Strips of sheet metal were then used to join the panels up to the drip rail on both the inside and outside of the rear window. The same was done at the windshield but this time only the inner section was joined together for reasons that will also become clearer at a later point in the operation.

■ As the rear panel extends upward toward the roof on either side of the rear window opening it also tapers. Since we removed a 2-1/2 inch section of this it was necessary to cut a slit down each vertical edge and weld it closed again to match up the taper from bottom to top.

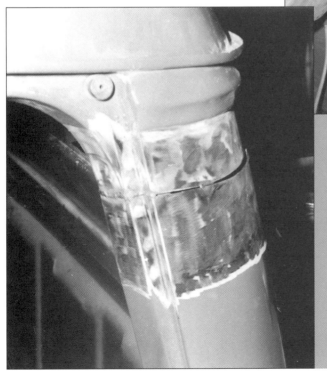

■ The pillar areas give the roof most of its strength and support so they are fully welded first. Notice how there is a small amount of misalignment in the panel as it curves around the back of the cabin. This will need to be corrected before we weld up the seam, as it is too great to be "worked out" as we go.

■ To correct the curvature of the lower section of this panel so that it more neatly aligns with the upper section, a vertical cut is made as shown. The resulting gap can then be pushed in to align and welded up again, tightening up the radius of the corner.

■ Here the entire corner panel has been welded up and the roof is beginning to look like a unit again. Note the generous use of body filler that needs to be cleaned well back from the weld areas to prevent it from burning as you weld. The entire body will be stripped and redone as the truck undergoes its full rebuild.

■ Next we get into the really tricky part of this top chop, the windshield opening. The upper edge of the windshield opening needs to be modified extensively to enable us to keep the windshield glass as stock as possible. For this reason only the inner support skin is welded back together at this point when we joined the two halves of the roof. Spot welds across the lip of the opening were then drilled out and the leading edge or "eyebrow" of the roof panel cut off as shown here.

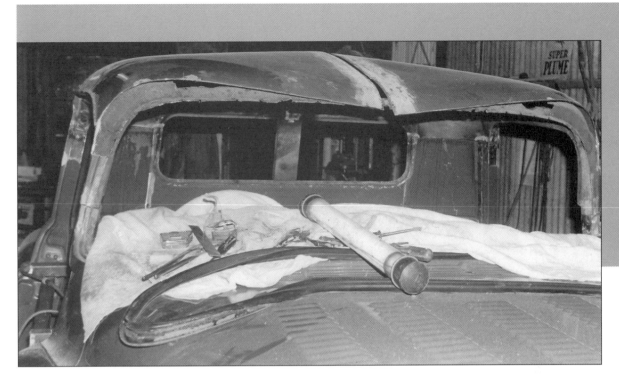

■ This leaves the front edge of the roof very forlorn looking but there's good reason for it, just stay with us for the full story. Note how the inner rail of the windshield opening is still intact at this point, but as yet the windshield pillars aren't welded in place.

■ Back to cutting again! This time we have marked out the one inch wide section of the turret that is then cut out to create a flatter roofline that will compliment the new lowered profile of the truck. Yes, doing the chop this way did create a lot of welding but the end result was well worth it.

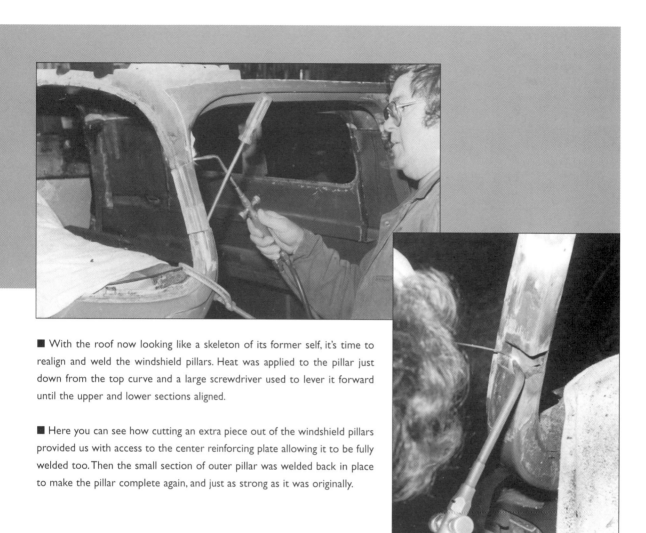

■ With the roof now looking like a skeleton of its former self, it's time to realign and weld the windshield pillars. Heat was applied to the pillar just down from the top curve and a large screwdriver used to lever it forward until the upper and lower sections aligned.

■ Here you can see how cutting an extra piece out of the windshield pillars provided us with access to the center reinforcing plate allowing it to be fully welded too. Then the small section of outer pillar was welded back in place to make the pillar complete again, and just as strong as it was originally.

■ The windshield glass is now put back into position using just the lower section of its rubber. This gives us a clear indication of how much lower the roofline will be and allows us to assess how much reshaping of the upper windshield opening will be required.

■ A length of masking tape is used to provide a reference point on the glass where the top edge of the windshield opening will need to align. This piece of tape was left in place on the glass as it will also serve as a rough guide for cutting the new laminated windshield that will be used in the finished article.

■ Part Two will show you the rest of the chopping operation. Here the main inner rail of the windshield opening has been cut at each end, moved forward until it contacts the glass at our reference line and with just its own rubber lip cut from the original windshield rubber fitted in between. That should leave it sitting exactly as it would when the glass is cut down and fitted into the new opening. The length of upper lip is then lightly clamped into place as shown and we can start work on reshaping the top forward section of the windshield pillars so that the entire opening conforms to the shape of the glass. Now you can see the reason for leaving the lower 2/3 of the windshield opening in its stock configuration.

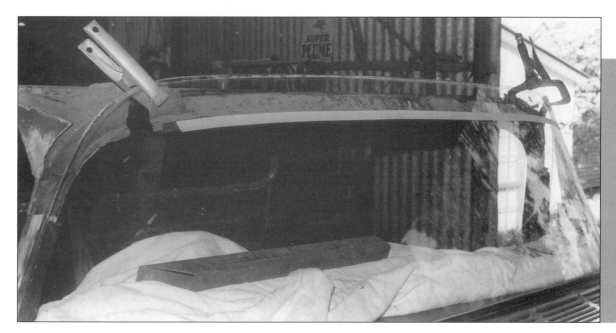

Modifying the windshield opening, sectioning the turret and chopping the doors.

WHEN WE LEFT YOU IN PART ONE WE HAD CUT THE remaining inner top lip of the windshield opening free from the body, moved it forward and lightly clamped it to the windshield glass in its new position. To keep it in this position a light gauge box tube framework was tack welded into the forward area of the now topless roof section. Three arms extend forward and were tack welded to the remaining inner windshield lip to keep it permanently in its new position once we removed the windshield glass again. Having done this we could then attack the upper corners of the windshield pillars to recontour them so that they followed the contour of the glass and once more joined up with the inner lip section.

This is more easily followed in the photos so we won't try to explain it any further here. Suffice to say that we had to split the pillars from the top and pull the front edge forward to the glass. This opened up a vee shaped gap that was then filled with sections of sheet metal. Small extra sections also had to be fabricated to gain extra length along the windshield opening lip so that it could all be joined into one piece again. As we proceeded with this tricky section we had to periodically sit the windshield in place again to make sure the recontoured lip conformed to the glass.

PART TWO

Once we had completed the recontouring of the inner lip all the way across the top of the windshield opening (several days work!), we could make a final check with the windshield in place. Then we could tackle the replacement of the roof "eyebrow" and the rest of the roof skin itself. With the eyebrow back in place it is no longer possible to sit the stock windshield in place and since we weren't modifying the glass ourselves, this was our last chance to make sure the opening was "right".

Replacing the eyebrow above the windshield was relatively straightforward up to a point. All we had to do was align the spot welds where we had separated them along the windshield lip working from the center outwards. However since we had to completely recontour the upper corners of the windshield opening, we naturally had to do the same to the outer ends of the eyebrow. This wasn't really all that difficult but it was very time consuming. Again it is easier to illustrate this step in photos.

Finally it's time to start reskinning the roof to make the cabin complete once more. Because the roof section spreads as it comes down the original skin needs to be separated into four individual pieces. When we cut the turret off we removed the extra one inch section along the sides and around the back of the roof but now that it's time to put it back on we also needed to remove a corresponding section of the front edge. The original roof has a less curved profile at this point so we needed to take a more substantial section off to keep all the original curved profiles in proportion with each other from front to back and from front to side.

With all the trimming completed each of the four sections were next welded into place along their outer edges leaving us with a fairly wide gap across the roof and a narrower gap running front to back. Filling in these gaps with sections of sheet metal makes the roof complete again but it wasn't as easy as it sounds. Heat shrinkage was a problem with so much welding required but we also had to contend with original roof sections that had been heavily skinned with filler. This made it difficult to judge whether the contour of the roof was correct and in the end we ground most of the filler away so that we could rework the entire roof skin into shape.

Even using the hammer welding method this operation was difficult until we had about three-quarters of the welding completed. The problem was not having enough support within the skin itself so we had to weld and stretch as we went to keep the panel somewhere near its original shape. With all the welding completed we then worked our way across the entire roof, stretching, shrinking and beating as we went. We only took the roof to a rough-finished state at this point as the entire body is to be redone during the course of a total rebuild.

Only one step remains in our top chopping operation, the door tops need to be chopped to fit back into their openings. As it turned out this was also the easiest step. Each door was marked out in a similar fashion to the roof and then the tops were cut off. This allows the door to close again and makes it easier to align them in their lowered profile. As with the roof section there was only about 1/4-inch misalignment at the front when the top sections of the doors were refitted. Heat was applied to the front top corner and the upright section was realigned and welded. The doors also have an inner trim strip, that extends around the window opening sides. This was simply shortened at the bottom ends and clipped back into position. It was flexible enough to conform to the slightly altered profile of the door top without needing to be heated and stretched.

That completes the entire operation as carried out in our workshop. From here it went back to Peter Collier's own garage in Canberra where the rest of the rebuild was undertaken. Because the windshield glass has such compound curves it was shortened by sandblasting away the required amount. Despite the care taken to make the windshield conversion as easy as possible, two windshields were broken in the blasting process before a successful third one was completed.

■ A temporary framework was tack welded into the forward area of the cabin to hold the inner lip of the windshield opening in place against the glass. This allows the clamps to be removed and the glass to be taken away but still leave the lip in its new position. Now the recontouring of the outer corners can begin.

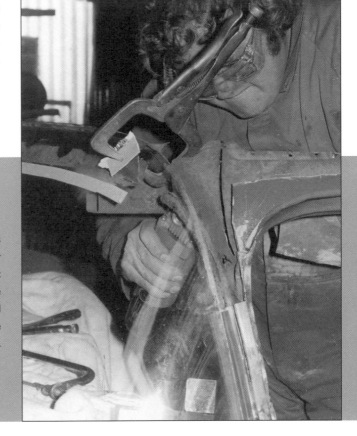

■ First step in the recontouring process was to split the windshield pillar working down from the top to about halfway down the pillar. This allows the forward section of the pillar to be pulled forward to follow the contour of the windshield glass at its new lower height.

■ Pulling the front half of the pillar forward opens up a V shaped gap which then needs to be filled in with sheet metal. In this case we had to reshape the upper section of the pillar so that the roof skin would clear it and in so doing were able to use the original metal to fill in the outer V gap (white arrows). Previous accident damage had badly affected the lip that holds the windshield rubber (black arrows) at this corner so it was remade at the same time.

■ This view from inside the pillar shows the recontouring of the left side corner completed. Note how pieces of sheet metal have been added in to fill the roughly Vee-shaped gap created when the forward section of the pillar was pulled towards the glass.

■ Now is the last chance to check the shape of the new opening against the original uncut windshield glass before we start replacing the outer "eyebrow" and reskinning the roof. Once the eyebrow is back in place it is no longer possible to fit the uncut windshield glass.

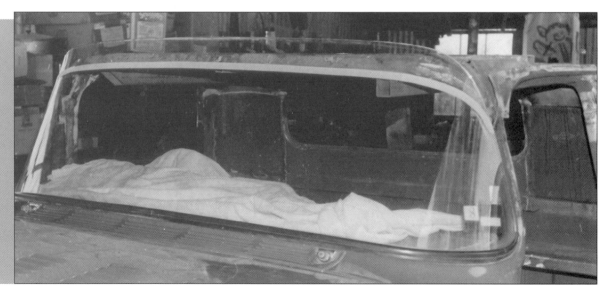

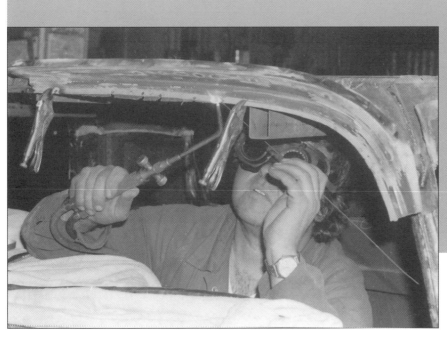

■ Refitting this section of the eyebrow is relatively easy as we only had to realign the original spot welds where they were separated and weld them up again. However it is already evident that the outer corner will have to be reworked to follow the new contour of the inner windshield opening panel.

■ To do this several hacksaw cuts were made at the corner to allow the radius of the curve to be tightened, This was done progressively, pulling the eyebrow into the new shape as we went. Vertical cuts were also needed at the lower end to allow this section to be tapered back into the windshield pillar so that the whole corner looked "factory original".

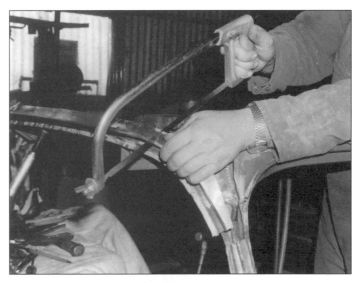

■ A small piece of sheet metal was used to fill in the remaining gap on the upper outside of the pillar giving us a "squared up" corner to work to as the roof skin is refitted.

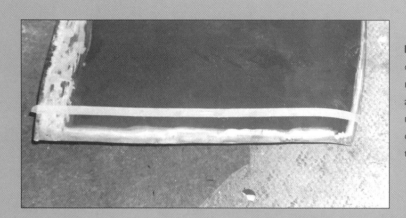

■ To take the corresponding one inch of vertical height out of the front of the roof panel we had to remove the amount shown here as the contour is more gentle at this point than it was down the sides and rear. At this point in time the roof skin was still two halves.

■ Next step was to cut these panels in half again giving us a roof skin that is now four quarters.

■ Each corner is then welded in place at the front and rear leaving gaps across the middle of the roof from side to side and front to back.

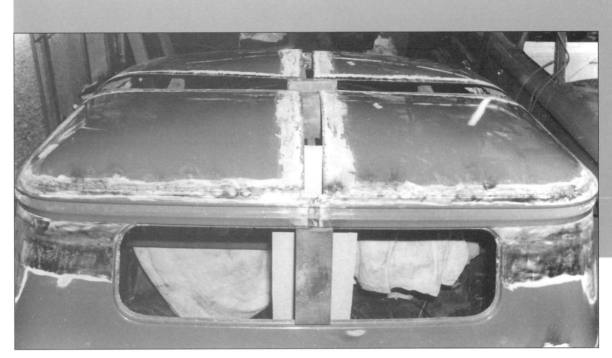

■ This view of the roof panels in place gives a clear picture of how much filling-in will be needed to make the roof complete again, Having a second roof available would have made this step easier but we didn't have access to a spare roof! Note the block of wood in the center of the rear window to prevent the window opening pulling inward as welding on the roof takes place.

■ The side view gives an indication of the new flatter roofline taking shape. Note supports also used in the center of the windshield opening to prevent it from pulling in as the skin is welded back in place.

■ Now comes the difficult part - filling in the gaps with sheet metal. The front to rear gap was filled in first using the hammer welding method, then the side to side gap was filled a piece at a time starting from the outer edges.

■ Having to fill in such large areas was quite difficult as distortion was a constant problem until the roof was all one piece again and regained some rigidity. We had to mercilessly beat the roof from underneath to stretch it into shape once the welding was completed and then shrink back areas to even out the whole panel.

■ Our job wasn't made any easier by the presence of a more than adequate amount of filler from previous body repairs. In fact the whole body had been skimmed with plastic filler. In order to get the panel relatively even we found it necessary to sand away most of the filler and then work over the whole roof panel with slapping iron and dolly.

■ After many hours work the roof is now complete again. Some residue of filler still remains and the black spots indicate where shrinkage was carried out but it's all basically even again ready for final bodywork preparation. The whole truck was to be rebuilt so this is as far as we went with the finishing off work at this stage. Only the doors remain to be chopped.

■ Bolting the stock door in place graphically illustrates how much the top has been chopped. Pieces of masking tape indicate where the cuts will be made to shorten the door. They correspond with where the cuts were made in the roof pillars.

■ The hacksaw was used to cut the top section off the door which can now be closed in its stock position again. Everything has remained in alignment thanks to our internal frame.

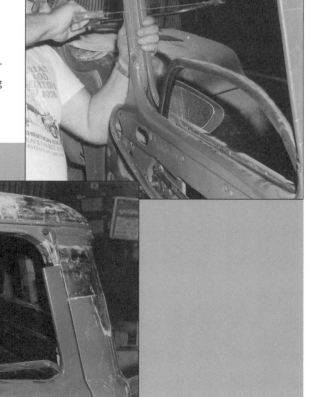

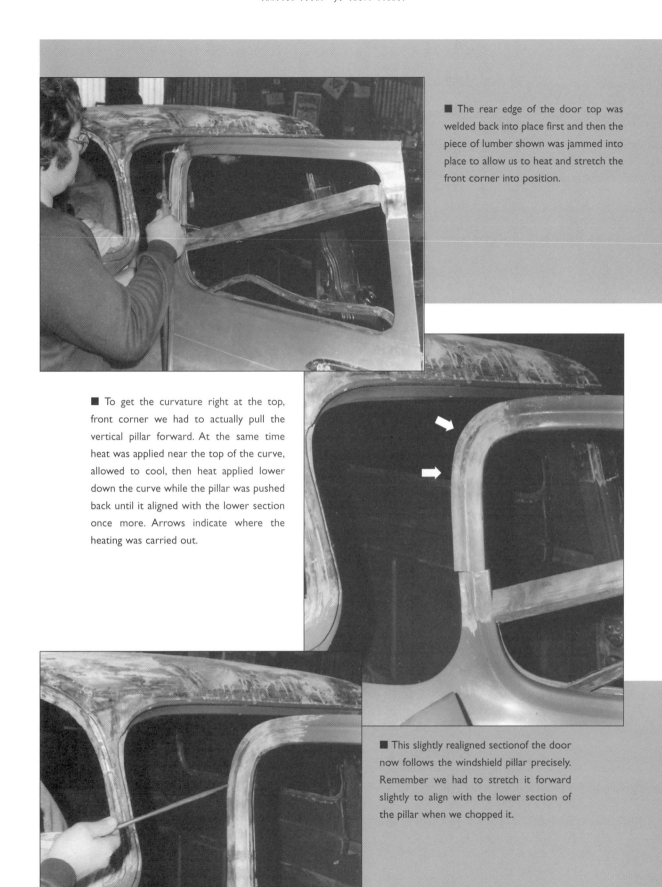

■ The rear edge of the door top was welded back into place first and then the piece of lumber shown was jammed into place to allow us to heat and stretch the front corner into position.

■ To get the curvature right at the top, front corner we had to actually pull the vertical pillar forward. At the same time heat was applied near the top of the curve, allowed to cool, then heat applied lower down the curve while the pillar was pushed back until it aligned with the lower section once more. Arrows indicate where the heating was carried out.

■ This slightly realigned sectionof the door now follows the windshield pillar precisely. Remember we had to stretch it forward slightly to align with the lower section of the pillar when we chopped it.

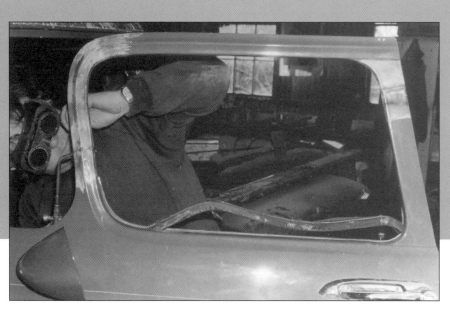

■ Welding up the aligned front sections of the door completes the basic chopping operation. No extra pieces had to be added into the doors to get them to align with their lowered openings. Quarter windows will be left out and the doors converted to one-piece glass design to clean up the side profile of the truck.

■ The upper doors have a trim panel that extends around the window opening on three sides. This was shortened by cutting off the ends as shown and redrilling to accept the mounting screw at each end. No reshaping of these trim panels was necessary as they are flexible enough to pull into shape as they are clipped into place.

■ It took several tries to sandblast the top of the windshield glass down to the required height but the end result fits perfectly as shown at right.

■ Back on the ground and out in the light on its own wheels the pickup displays its new overall profile to great advantage. The rear window retains a slight curve and a replacement will be cut from an existing (damaged) late model Japanese van type laminated windshield. Original type mounting rubber will be used to hold it in place. All glass cutting was done back in Canberra where the owner completely disassembled the truck for a ground up rebuild.

TOP CHOPPING AN EARLY FALCON SEDAN DELIVERY IS no small task. They are a fairly simple vehicle in design but there is an enormous amount of sheet metal in that delivery roof. These early Falcon deliveries used a windshield that is the same as the normal four door sedan, but other models, notably the hard top versions and Sprints used a shorter windshield. Using one of these shorter windshields and lowering the sedan delivery roof height to suit seemed to be the most common sense way to achieve a chopped delivery without creating too many problems when it comes time to fit it with glass. Using that theory we set out to compare the height of the two windshields. Measuring a hard top with its windshield in place seemed to indicate that there was a three inch difference between the two and we started to plan accordingly. Fortunately we checked more closely before actually embarking on the top chop as we discovered an important difference. In particular we had to revise the amount that we intended to chop the top.

Before we go any further I should point out that the sedan delivery shown in this chapter is an Australian version which is slightly different to the American early Falcon. However all the theory and most of the practical aspects of this top chopping operation will still be relevant.

When we measured the difference between the original windshield opening of the delivery and a hard top windshield, we came up with a figure of three inches. However in the course of measuring and marking out our delivery body in preparation for the actual chop, we did some more careful checking. This time we used sections of an old delivery windshield rubber to hold the glass in the position it actually goes and found that the amount the roof would have to be chopped to suit was only two inches, not three as we thought at first. More on the actual mechanics of this as we get further into this chapter.

We didn't mention it in the introduction to this chapter but another change we had intended to make was at the rear of the body. Normally when a roof that has slanting pillars is chopped it must be lengthened and widened so that it will mate up with the original pieces once more. At the rear of our delivery body this would have meant adding a section in across the roof so that the top of the rear window would finish up back in its original position in relation to the window glass. To overcome the need

for adding in this strip across the roof we had intended to slant the window forward more by leaning the rear pillars forward to suit. There is room inside the tailgate to allow the glass to fit at a greater angle but on closer inspection we found that while the glass channel sections could be moved to suit, the mechanism that drives it all could not be moved and so this part of the scheme had to be abandoned. However we did come up with a clever solution to the problem that still overcame the need to add in a strip across the roof. Once again we will explain this further as we progress.

Now let's retrace our steps a little and go back to the beginning of the actual work. We did completely strip the delivery down to a bare shell. Having done that we then set to and made up a rotisserie to support the body so that it could be worked on from any angle during the course of the rebuild. Next the body was manhandled to an open area in our back yard, mounted in the rotisserie and rotated 90° in readiness for the sandblaster.

PART ONE

It would be fair to say that the sandblaster was delighted with the rotisserie idea as it certainly made his work much easier, and quicker, which meant a saving for us. The entire underside of the delivery was blasted, together with the engine bay and door jambs. We knew there was very little rust in the delivery and the sandblasting didn't reveal any more than we had expected. It did however make it much easier to repair those sections that were rust damaged.

Even though we are chopping the top on our delivery body a full separate chassis won't be required. These early Falcons, particularly '64 and '65 models had quite substantial subframes and bulkheads built into them so it was only deemed necessary

■ The sedan delivery shown in this chapter is an Australian version which is slightly different to the American early Falcon. However all the theory and most of the practical aspects of this top chopping operation will still be relevant. Note that this Australian version uses a four door sedan door rather than the longer two door item used on the American Falcon delivery.

■ When we measured the difference between the original windshield opening of the delivery and a hard top windshield we came up with a figure of three inches. However in the course of measuring and marking out our delivery body in preparation for the actual chop, we did some more careful checking. This time we used sections of an old delivery windshield rubber to hold the glass in the position it actually goes and found that the amount the roof would have to be chopped to suit was only two inches, not three as we thought at first.

to strengthen these subframes and connect the front one to the rear. This was done by stitch welding reinforcing plates to the bottom of the subframes from front to rear. A MIG welder was used for this operation and while we were at it triangulated reinforcing plates were added at the front corners where the front strut rod mounts are located and all the critical factory welds around suspension mounts etc. were fully rewelded. Further strength was added by stitch welding the subframes to the floor.

Toward the rear of the body the front and rear subframes pass parallel to each other for a short distance but they don't actually connect. It was obvious that to connect these two together would greatly enhance the strength of the vehicle. We did this by building a "torque box" on each side out of steel plate. In effect connecting the subframes together in this manner virtually provides the body with a complete chassis that is built into its substructure.

Having completed the process of strengthening the underside of the vehicle we could now turn our attention to the top chopping operation. The first step in this part of the operation was to build an internal framework to hold the body rigidly in position while the roof is removed. The last thing you want to happen when you remove the roof is to have the various sections of the body move around and therefore out of alignment when you put the roof back on again! At the rear we used part of our rotisserie to form the rearmost section of the inner framework. At the front, connectors join the top door hinge mount with the door latch area and cross braces connect each side. Two long rails then connect all this from front to back as shown in the photos and an X member in the center of the cargo area adds even more strength. This may seem like a lot of work but the benefits are well worth the extra effort.

Now we're almost ready to slice the roof off the delivery but there are a few other minor details to take care of first. There are several lateral braces on the underside of the roof that connect from one side to the other and provide support for the expanse of sheet metal that forms the roof skin. These were all carefully removed and set aside. They will later be modified and refitted to the chopped body. The same applies to two vertical braces on each side of the cargo area that hold a wooden support against the upper side panels.

Before marking out the roof for chopping it was time to once again bring out our two door windshield and mock it into position for accurate measurements to be taken. This time we used small sections of an original delivery windshield rubber to hold the windshield in its true position. Doing this revealed the difference in the anticipated chop we would perform as

mentioned at the start of this chapter. When we first sized things up with the two door windshield we simply sat it in place in the empty windshield opening without using any rubber. However when we used the small sections of rubber to hold it in place it soon became evident that there would be quite a difference. You can never be too careful when carrying out an exercise like this and it pays to check and check again before you actually start chopping. With the pieces of windshield rubber in place it is immediately obvious (see photos) that the bottom edge of the windshield is actually supported above the lip of the windshield opening while at the top the edge of the glass sits ahead of the lip and slightly above it. In effect the windshield rubber profile is different top to bottom and the sides are different again. Having allowed for all this and remeasured everything we came up with an actual height difference of two inches instead of the three inches we had measured when the windshield was positioned in the opening without any rubber.

With the windshield supported in position by the sections of windshield rubber it is now quite obvious where the top corners of the two door windshield will need to be modified to suit the lowered delivery opening. However before grinding the windshield to shape we will proceed with the top chop. If you intend carrying out a similar chop on any vehicle make sure you consult the person who will be modifying your glass before you get too far into the job. Often it is better to chop the opening and only tack it into position until the glass is modified and you can be sure it will fit the opening. Sometimes it is easier to make minor adjustments to the metalwork than it is to make the glass fit the finished opening. If it is only tacked in position these changes can be made easily, but if you've already finished all the metal work any further changes to make the glass fit can mean a lot of effort has been wasted. We had our local windshield expert check out our delivery before we cut anything and in this case he was confident the opening could be chopped and the glass ground to suit without any problems.

Having dealt with the windshield and its proposed modifications it was time to start marking out the roof prior to actually chopping it. A word of advice here for any aspiring top chopper - measure twice (or more) and cut once. In fact on this particular project we spent the best part of two days working out the windshield modifications and measuring the top for the chop. A lot of thought means less physical work and a cleaner finished job.

The roof section of a second sedan delivery escaped unscathed when that vehicle was extensively damaged in an accident. Having two roofs to work with on a project like this is a great advantage. By measuring the amount the roof would

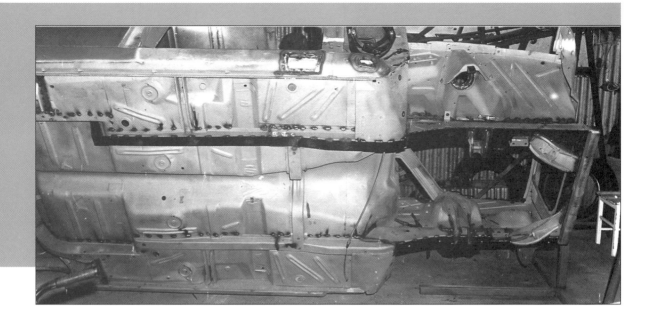

■ With our delivery mounted in a rotisserie it was much easier to carry out strengthening modifications to the underside. Steel strips were stitch welded to all the subframe members and the subframes themselves were stitch welded to the floor. The front subframes were also tied to the rear subframes to essentially give the vehicle a complete chassis welded into the sub-structure. It is now much stronger than it was originally. At right the rear rotisserie mount is being fitted into the tailgate mounts.

■ Having reinforced all the underside it's now time to turn our attention to the top chop. The first stage of this operation is to build an extensive reinforcing framework inside the vehicle to hold everything in place while the roof is removed. Notice here how the door hinge and latch mounts have been used as attachment points for the framework.

need to spread as it comes down we were able to use the two roofs each cut "overcenter" by half the corresponding difference and end up with only one weld right down the center of the vehicle. At the sides the cut was made about a third of the way down the side panel where access to the inside was easy. The photos that accompany this chapter will obviously tell the story better than words.

Not only does the roof have to spread across its width as it comes down. It also needs to move forward and rearward to compensate for the slanting pillars. It's here that our project co-worker Harry Wright came up with a brilliant idea! Since we had already established that we couldn't lean the rear window forward to avoid adding in a strip across the back of the roof, as mentioned earlier in this article, Harry suggested that we simply move the entire roof rearwards to make up the difference! In actual fact it turned out that we only needed to move the whole thing back some 7/8 of an inch and the idea worked perfectly. Of course this meant the upper door pillar was also moved rearward the same amount but here we were able to use some of the two inch section we removed to rebuild the top of the door pillar in its original configuration and thus retain all of its original strength. Not only were we able to do that but in so doing we were also able to fully weld all the sections of metal that make up this important area of strength in the body from inside and out.

Of course the front section of the roof has to be extended forward to compensate for the slant of the windshield pillars too. To accomplish this, using our two roof sections, a cut was made at an angle from just forward of the center door pillar across to a point just to the rear of the top of the windshield opening. By carefully calculating all this we were able to use opposite sides of the sections of roof used for the major part of the project and have them butt together with only one join at the top center of the windshield opening. The only extra piece of metal that has to be added as a result of chopping the roof in this manner is a piece three inches long and one and a half inches wide near the center front of the roof (see photos).

The four major parts that now comprise our new roof were welded in position at the pillars and where they butt together at the center rear and center front. This allowed us to once again sit our two door windshield in place and confirmed that it was all going to fit as planned, a major concern dealt with successfully. Now we can turn our attention to zipping it all back together again.

While many would proclaim that the best way to weld large areas of sheet metal like this back together would be to use a MIG welder we elected to do ours with gas. However you will need some experience to tackle a similar project yourself or you could end up with warpage problems. Even using a MIG welder on such large flat sections of sheet metal won't guarantee that warpage won't occur. The idea is to keep it to a minimum. We started with the side panels which had been prepared so that the butting line where they were to be joined was a nice flush fit. This is imperative for a good welding job. The entire length of the join was first tack welded together using tacks spaced about 3/4 inch apart. That may seem unnecessarily close together but for welding in the manner that we did, the closer together the tacks are the better and easier the final welding operation becomes.

Once tacked along the entire length of the side we then went back and started at one end and fuse welded the whole length together in one operation. No hammering was carried out at all until the entire side was welded up. This is different to the more common practice of hammer welding along such a join. In that process a short length is welded, then hammered flat with a dolly behind, while it is still glowing red. This method works quite well but does put tension into the panel and work hardens the weld area as you progress. By using our tacking and fuse welding method the entire work area remains soft and malleable and can then be beaten into shape quite easily. In fact if the panel fit is very good and the welding smooth and continuous very little warpage will result anyway, especially when the panel being welded is well supported at each end as was the case here.

Once we had completed the weld along the side, a slapping iron and dolly was used to work over the welded panel and a beating hammer was only used on sections that needed a little extra work. Ours turned out very nicely and will only need a little extra work before it can be prepared for paint.

Attention now turns to the top of the roof. Here we began by tack welding the angled joins from the top of the door opening across to the top of the windshield. These were left tacked together while we do the same to the long join right down the center of the vehicle. In this case we started at the rear and worked our way forward. Because the roof itself is such a large unsupported area we finish welded these joins using the hammer welding method so that we added rigidity as we went. It's impossible to weld such a large, flat and thin panel without creating some distortion but a few hours in the hands of a competent panel beater and you will never pick how the roof was chopped!

The only remaining job to be carried out was to weld in the small rectangular piece of metal at the center front and once more our delivery bodyshell is back in one piece, albeit two inches shorter.

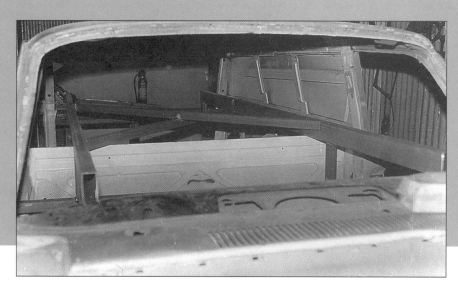

■ This view through the windshield opening shows how the two main rails extend from front to rear and are joined together with a large X member. The whole framework is virtually a temporary chassis within the car.

■ The rear view shows how the framework was attached to the rotisserie mounts in the tailgate area. Once the top chop is completed the entire framework will be removed from the car but the rotisserie will be left intact.

■ All the roof supports were removed from inside the vehicle to make it easier to cut the roof apart. These will be widened to suit the lower roof line and put back in place once the top chop is completed.

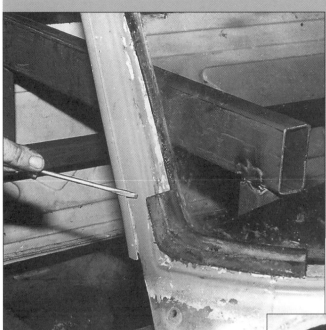

■ Using small sections of an original delivery windshield rubber to hold the glass in position it quickly became apparent that the difference in height isn't as great as first thought. Note how the rubber actually supports the bottom edge of the glass above the lip of the windshield opening. The cross section of the rubber is actually different top and bottom and different again at the sides.

■ Now you can see that the difference in height is actually two inches, not three. This photo also illustrates how the top corners of the hard top windshield have a slightly different shape to the sedan delivery opening.

■ Spirit level and tape measure were used to accurately measure the exact difference in height vertically. We did this two or three times to make sure we had it right.

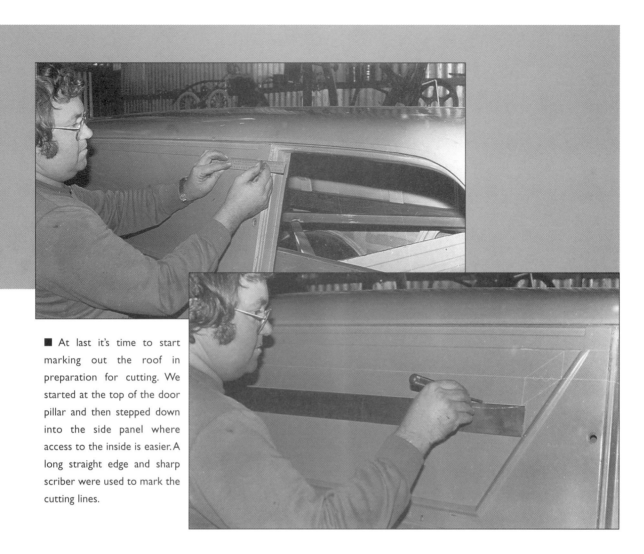

■ At last it's time to start marking out the roof in preparation for cutting. We started at the top of the door pillar and then stepped down into the side panel where access to the inside is easier. A long straight edge and sharp scriber were used to mark the cutting lines.

■ These photos show where the lines were scribed in the door pillar area of the delivery and at the rear pillars. A lot of time, measuring and thought at this point can save you a lot of work later. In fact we spent almost two days measuring and marking out the delivery before we made a single cut. Notice how the cut lines pass through the corners of the body pressings which makes them much easier to realign as the top comes down.

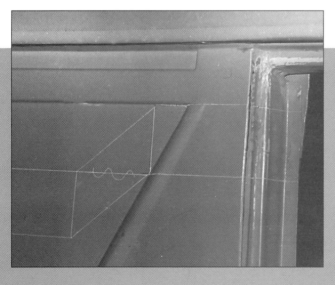

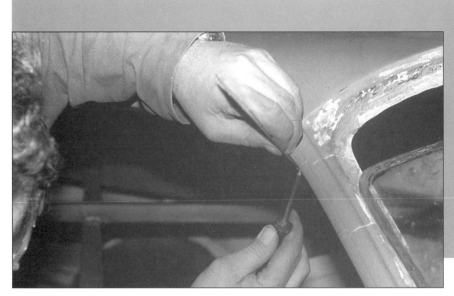

■ The windshield pillar is to be cut as close as possible to the top corner. At this point it is important to remember that we are taking out two inches vertically. You may need to recall some of your maths education to calculate the correct amount of pillar to be removed to give an end result of two inches vertically!

■ Having marked out our sedan delivery body in preparation for the chop it's now time to do the same on the old accident damaged original "donor" body. Since we only need parts of the roof panel off this body we only need to mark the upper line and cut at that point.

■ Once again a long straight edge is used to scribe the cutting lines onto the panel. Our calculations indicated that the roof needs to "spread" 3/4 of an inch as it comes down so each half of the roof panel to be used was marked out 3/8 of an inch overcenter. Using two roofs enables us to do this and end up with only one seam down the center of the vehicle.

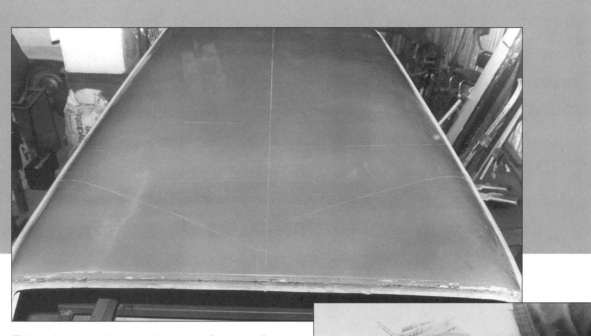

■ At the front edge of each roof section our "overcenter" parting line needs to step to the opposite side of the vehicle. Doing this leaves us with a long wide main roof panel from each roof, but from opposite sides, that eventually will be joined together to form the new roof. In order to get the entire new roof from only two originals we need to use the opposite sides at the front, cut at an angle as shown so that the four new panels butt together. To get a better understanding of the whole process study the photo above and then visualise the second roof cut in the opposite manner to this one. Simple huh!

■ At long last it's time to actually start cutting the roof off. Before we did start cutting though we left the project overnight to allow all our theory to recycle through our minds just in case we had overlooked something. A double check next morning confirmed that we hadn't and so the hacksaw was put to work on the windshield pillars.

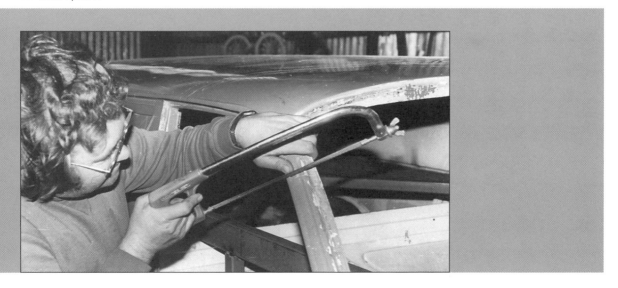

■ A hacksaw was used to cut the main pillars where in some cases there are several sections of metal to cut through. There is also a fairly substantial metal brace across the back of the roof so that too was cut with the hacksaw.

■ The rest of the cuts through the large panels were made with a cut-off wheel in a hand grinder. Notice how the cut shown here is the lower one. This is the only one needed on this section because the top part on this side will be discarded.

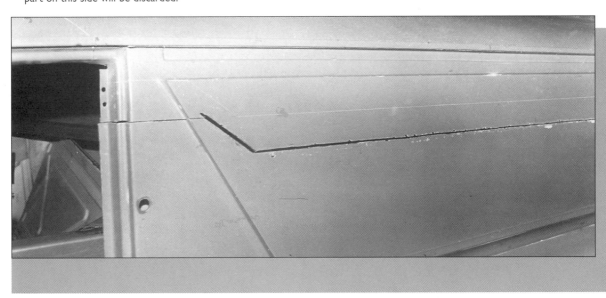

■ With the whole roof removed you can see how important it is to fit the interior framework to keep the remainder of the vehicle from moving around.

■ It is also much easier to cut the two roof panels into their various sections once they are removed from the vehicle,

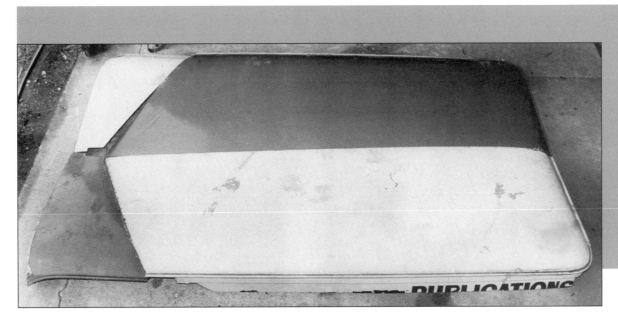

■ The four sections that will make up the new roof can be mocked together to show how the end result will be achieved. By cutting the roof in the manner described in this article the only additional piece of metal required is a small rectangular piece at the center front. The length of this section indicates how much longer the new roof is compared to the original roof.

■ Hardest part of the whole operation so far was balancing the sections of roof so that they could be refitted to the vehicle. Once in position the butting edges were checked for fit and alignment before tack welding the major pillars was undertaken.

■ A piece of light box tube was clamped in place across the back edge of the roof and this braced section was joined with fairly substantial tack welds.

■ Having the roof joined at the back then allowed any further minor adjustments to be made for accurate panel fit.

■ Because we moved the whole roof rearwards as explained in the text some adjustments were necessary at the door pillar. In particular the top of the door pillar itself also moves rearward but this was corrected by removing the original piece and replacing it with part of the two inch section that was removed in the chop.

■ At the rear the pillar meets up again very nicely but a 7/8 inch vertical section has to be removed where indicated to allow for the rearward movement of the roof as it came down.

■ Back to the door pillar to show you how the replacement section of pillar was refitted to the roof rail, maintaining this important area of strength. You can also see how we had access to the inside of the pillar to enable it to be fully welded in place

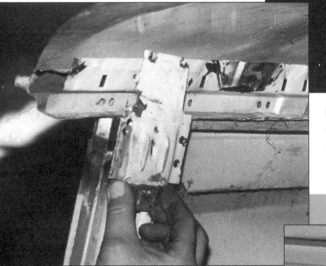

■ Now the original top inner section of the pillar can be trimmed to size and refitted leaving the pillar in the same configuration as it was originally but two inches shorter.

■ Once again back to the outside of the pillar where a small section of the two inch piece that was removed is now used to fill in the outer sheetmetal so that it all looks standard again.

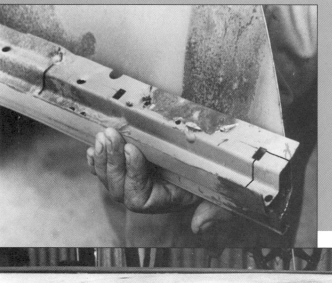

■ Fitting the front sections of roof is now fairly straight forward but there is one important aspect to take into consideration. The roof itself prevents access to the inside section of the side roof rail so a small section is removed where marked to give us access to the inside for welding. Later this small section will be welded back in place.

■ Now the front section can be tack welded in place at the top of the windscreen pillar and at the join just forward of the door pillar. The join at the center top of the windshield opening can now also be tack welded to make our roof basically complete again.

■ Having tacked the sections of roof in position it is now time to trial fit the windshield once again. Now it becomes quite obvious how much difference there is at the top corners but the rest of the screen will fit perfectly. At this stage we checked with our windshield fitter again to make sure he thought it was okay to proceed with welding up the entire roof.

■ Where the pillars and centre front and rear were previously only tack welded into position they can now be fully welded prior to welding up all the long seams. The rectangular hole left at the centre front is now clearly obvious.

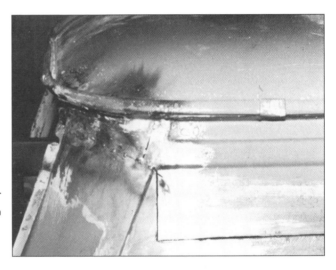

■ With the inner pillars fully welded the outer sheetmetal can now be tack welded into position leaving only the long cuts to be dealt with.

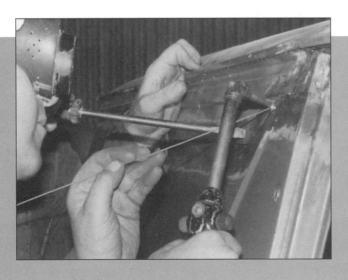

■ The sides were tack welded from front to back using tacks about 3/4 inch apart. A large screwdriver and a second pair of hands are useful at this point to keep the two pieces of sheetmetal aligned as you go.

■ On completion of the tack welding process we went back to one end and fuse welded the two panels together right along the entire side. If the fit is good and the tack welds close enough together no filler rod is necessary apart from where minor "blowholes" might occur. No hammering is needed either until the entire seam is finished (see text for details).

■ Our attention now turns to the top itself where we begin by tack welding the join that runs from the door pillar to the centre front of the roof.

■ Before attempting to tack weld the longest seam right down the centre of the roof we made up this simple "buck" to hold the panels up in position while they are tacked together.

■ Because these top seams are so long and for most part unsupported, we decided to hammer weld them so that the general shape of the roof was better able to be maintained as we went.

■ Here it is all welded back together and with our small rectangular opening at the front finally filled in. Chopping a roof that consists of such a large area of sheetmetal is no easy task but we're sure you will agree ours has turned out fairly well. In Part Two we'll show the replacement of the roof reinforcing members and the modifications to the windshield.

The Finishing Details – modifying and fitting the roof bows, chopping the doors, modifying the glass.

PART ONE OF THIS CHAPTER CONTAINED A comprehensive report on how the subframes of our van were turned into a reinforced, built-in chassis prior to the top being chopped. This time round we finish off the top chopping operation, chop the doors as well and modify our hard top windshield to fit the lowered sedan delivery opening.

Having fully welded all the seams of our 'new' lowered roof we were ready to beat it into shape. Such a large unsupported area of sheet metal consumed quite a deal of time to get it back into its original shape and once we had it roughly 2/3 done we found we had to refit the inside roof bows to hold it in position as we worked from back to front. Before we could refit the bows though they also had to be cut and lengthened to suit the new wider roof. This was easily done using two 'long halves' to make each new bow, but one of them has provision for the interior light so it was lengthened by adding a piece either side of the light pressing. We're not sure at this stage whether we will use the original type interior light but at least it's in place if we do.

PART TWO

Once we had beaten the roof completely into shape we found that the very front edge above the windshield had distorted and looked untidy. To remedy this we cut it through with a hacksaw up into the roof about six inches, used a small hydraulic jack to push and hold it in the right position and rewelded this section. This evened the windshield opening out nicely and left it ready for the final fitting up of the windshield.

Before tackling the windshield itself we turned our attention to the doors which at this stage were still in standard configuration. Careful measurements were taken and the door tops marked out as shown in the photo ready for cutting. By doing this part of the operation in the manner shown here we were able to chop the door tops without needing extra material from donor doors. Study the photos and captions carefully to see how this was achieved. Our internal frame that was fitted into the vehicle to hold it all in shape during the top chopping operation was removed prior to chopping the doors.

The final part of our operation this time round was to modify our hard top windshield so that it fits the lowered sedan delivery opening. The hard top windshield is the right curvature but the top corners have a 'squarer' shape than the original sedan delivery glass. To overcome this we ordered a laminated hard top windshield with tinted band across the top and had a windshield expert grind the corners to the sedan delivery opening shape. This is a delicate task that should only be attempted by an experienced operator and even then it's usually an 'all care but no responsibility' type of deal.

We first sat the new windshield in place in the opening using small sections of an original van windshield rubber to hold it in its correct location. Masking tape was then used to create a guide line for grinding to, but it's still a 'careful as she goes' operation with a trial fit between each session of grinding. Ours worked out very well and in fact only consumed about two hours. To get the hard top glass to fit the van opening the corner had to he ground to a 'rounder' shape and a tapering piece ground off towards the center of the windshield and also down the ends from the top towards the bottom. Once the grinding process was completed we then worked on the lip of the sedan delivery opening to make sure it conformed to the glass uniformly all the way round. With this completed the new windshield was stored away in a secure place until it is needed again later in the project.

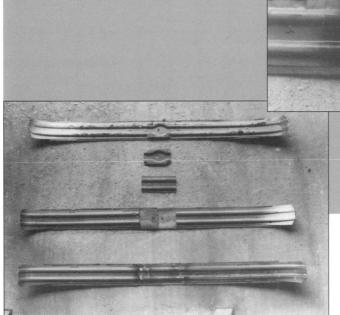

■ Having two sets of steel roof support bows made it easy to make up one widened set to suit the new lower roof line. Some were widened by simply cutting two halves over center and butt welding the long halves back together. One of the bows has provision for the interior light pressed into it so it was widened by adding a section either side of the light pressing. Other bows included the light pressing even though it isn't used and in these cases a plain section was used in the center to make the new, wider bow. We aren't sure if we will actually use the standard interior light but it is in place if we do. Each bow has a padding along its top side and this was retained in all cases.

■ Starting from the rear of the vehicle each bow was successively tack welded back into position as the roof was beaten into shape. Such a large area of sheet metal needs the support underneath as you go, to hold it in place as you work forward, beating the roof into shape. its a long slow process and occasionally we had to go back and remove one bow to get each section just right. Note the small hydraulic jack used to hold pressure against the bow while it is welded into position.

■ Once we had beaten the roof into shape all over we found we had a short section at the top of the windshield opening that had distorted somewhat and needed further work. Rather than "just fill it later", we cut the section open again for a short distance into the roof to allow us to "work out" the distortion.

■ Our small hydraulic jack was used again here to hold the front edge of the windshield opening in position while our troublesome section was beaten into shape properly and welded up again. Now the whole roof is completely finished and only requires buffing off and a skin of body filler added to take out the minor irregularities. This we will do later in the project along with other bodywork.

■ At long last it's now time to remove our internal frame that held everything in place while we chopped the top. At times the framework got in the way but it is certainly the only way to chop a top and be sure that everything will fit back into place.

■ Time now to fit the doors to the body shell so that we can mark and chop their tops to suit the new roofline. This picture graphically shows the difference in height from the stock roofline. Even though the top was only chopped two inches the effect is dramatic.

■ The door tops were marked out as shown so that there would be as few joins as possible in the finished item. At the rear edge the cuts were made through the corner of the window and at the same angle two inches further down. This piece of the upright section is kept for later use on the other

side door and vice versa. At the front edge the piece was removed from the top of the straight sloping section just before it begins to curve towards the rear. More than two inches must be removed at this point to allow for the sloping pillar.

■ A hacksaw is used to make these cuts but care is needed to make sure that the cuts are very square so that the end fit is very neat.

■ With the top cut off the door it can now be closed fully and we start to get some idea of how the finished item will look. We will be leaving the quarter window out of our van for a cleaner 'one-piece' side window appearance.

■ The shortened top section of the door is next tack welded back into place at the front edge. Note how the curvature of the top is now different to that of the roof line. There is probably a complex mathematical reason for this as it is a common occurrence when chopping a top like this, even though it appears to defy explanation.

■ So, we won't even try to explain it, just heat and carefully rebend the corner to suit the new profile as shown at right The section to be bent only needs to he heated to a dull cherry red and is bent quite easily, a little at a time, all the way around the curve.

■ To get the curvature exactly right the corner needs to be actually slightly overbent as shown, then pulled back up to the horizontal position. This process is quite easy but take your time to make the fit exactly right.

■The final step is to lengthen the back edge so that it meets up with the corner of the door again. This is where we used the short vertical section removed from the other side door. Because we cut at an angle through the corner of the door this piece is already the right shape to fit, it just needs to be shortened slightly and welded right in.

■ This close up shot of the corner of the door shows more clearly how this small piece from the other side door is used to make up the required length. That completes the metal part of our top chopping operation, now it's over to the windshield.

■ We mentioned earlier how we intended to use a hard top windshield in our delivery but that some minor modification was required. This photo shows why. The hard top windshield is the right curvature and we chopped the top to suit its height in the center, however the two door screen has a 'squarer' shape at the corners that need to be reshaped.

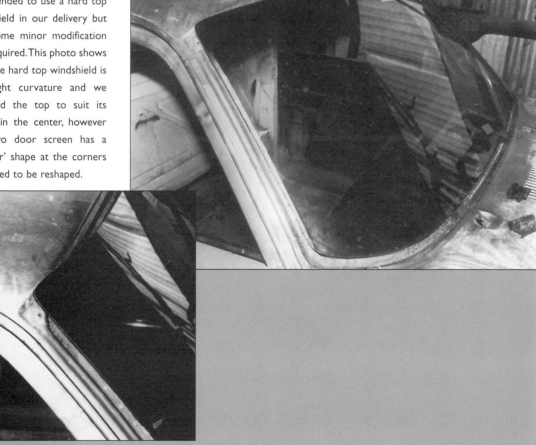

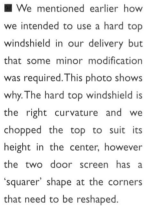

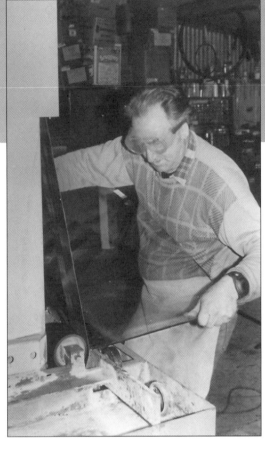

■ Masking tape is used to indicate where glass must be ground away from our laminated screen. This is exacting work and there aren't any second chances so caution is needed. Consequently we deliberately made the first mark so that the windshield would still need a little taken off it to fit properly. This way we can "sneak up" on the finished size rather than jump in too quick and make a mistake. A specialised sanding machine is used to grind down the glass a little at a time. The belt must always be in good cutting condition (changed regularly during the process) and is water lubricated and cooled. Let the glass get too hot or push too hard against a dull belt and your windshield is history. It's a case of 'all care but no responsibility' on the part of the operator.

■ After the first section is ground away across the top of the corner the windshield already looks as if it will fit. However there is still more work to do. In the process of grinding and checking our glass we had it in and out of the opening several times to make sure everything was right

■ Having ground away the top of the corner to allow the glass to fit right into the opening it is now evident that we need to remove a tapering section from the side of the glass. Once again masking tape is used as a guide for grinding.

■ Now that our glass has been ground to fit the opening, a little work is needed on the lip that holds the windshield rubber to make sure it conforms to the glass all the way around the opening. Once again this involves taking the glass in and out several times to make sure that everything is right.

■ Finally it's all finished and our "new" windshield is sitting in place using small sections of an original van windshield rubber. The hard top rubber is much different to the delivery item and can't be used. When the windshield is finally installed in the finished, painted van we will use a new repro delivery windshield rubber that will be cut and shortened to suit our chopped roofline. Although it was a fairly involved operation the entire process of reworking the corners of our hard top windshield to suit the delivery only took a little over two hours to complete.

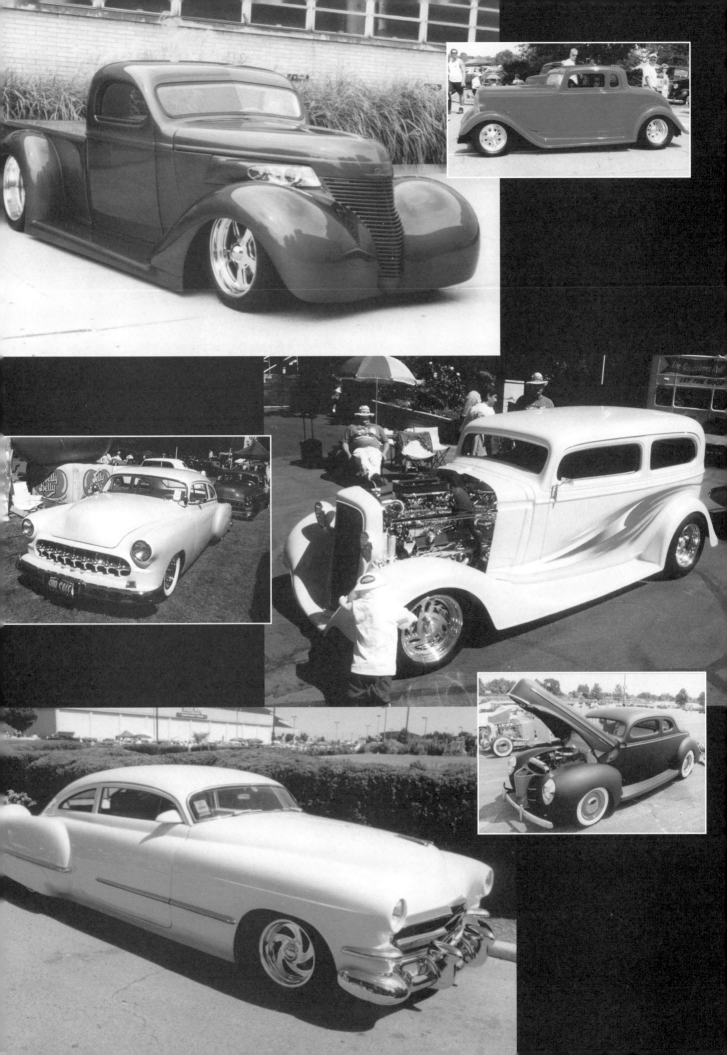

CHAPTER SIX
Fiberglass 1931 Ford Victoria

IT IS ONE THING TO BE ABLE TO CHOP THE TOP on a steel car but quite another to perform the same operation on a fiberglass body. Paul Kelly has wide experience in both types of work and in this chapter he shows us how he went about chopping the top on a fiberglass reproduction 1931 Model A Ford Victoria.

The popularity of fiberglass bodied hot rods is growing all the time and many of those bodies are closed car styles. While some are available from the manufacturer with the top already chopped, other body styles are supplied with a stock height roof. That was the situation with this Model A Victoria body.

While the body manufacturers are catering to this expanding market by producing stock and chopped versions of many body styles, each owner has different preferences, and none more so than the amount a top should be chopped. Even though your particular preference might be for a chopped body from one of the manufacturers, the amount of the chop may not suit your taste. In this chapter you will learn how to make it just the way you prefer.

PART ONE

Because of the material of construction used in these bodies, many owners are hesitant to modify them, or are unsure of the method required for joining the parts or finishing them off. They are often afraid of ruining the whole body. The sticky itching properties of the fiberglass materials can also be a deterrent to some enthusiasts.

The photographs in this chapter show the methods used to perform a chop on a fiberglass body. As with any job, the utmost care must be taken and all safety requirements related to the materials being used should be adhered to.

■ The rear view of the stock height '31 Vicky shows what an attractive body style it is even in standard form. Steel Victoria bodies are hard to find and often regarded as too valuable to cut up for a hot rod, but nobody will get too upset about chopping a fiberglass version.

■ The origin of this Victoria body was of Australian manufacture in the early '80s and was supplied as an unframed body with the doors, glass inner frames and outer skins unbonded. Previously the original owner made an attempt to steel out the body and set all panels. In all early bodies, either steel or glass, a skeleton frame of timber or steel is required to support and maintain rigidity. Due to the original builder's lack of experience (not enthusiasm), a large percentage of this steel frame had to be discarded and remanufactured.

■ This view shows that a steel box section had been incorporated in the forward section of the roof to house the stereo player, windshield wiper mechanism etc. Substantial gaps can be seen between the frame and the roof.

■ Before any work was commenced the door skins were trial fitted to check gaps and alignment. Keep a note book handy for drawing and measurements for reference later. Make sure the body is tightened down on the chassis before you begin cutting.

■ With every chop, picking the best place to make your cuts and minimise any misalignment is important. The methods of cutting is up to you, jigsaw, hacksaw, or fine cutting blade in an angle grinder can be used. Be prepared to replace cutting blades as the fiberglass will take the face off them quickly. At all times wear protective eyewear and a dust mask or respirator.

■ The cuts in the center door pillar were made halfway up the window opening and were quite straightforward.

■ To begin with just the sections of fiberglass were removed and the internal steel frame left intact.

■ At the windshield pillar the cuts were made at the top to allow for the tapered shape of the pillar itself.

■ As the frame and upper body were not bonded together it was a simple task to remove the roof.

■ The complete upper frame will be removed as a large amount of this structure is to be remade to conform more closely to the body's outer contours.

■ Even though this is an early body style the roof will still have to be lengthened to compensate for the leaning windshield pillars. Once we were happy with panel alignment the sections were secured in place using strips of aluminum and folded metal.

■ The same method was used to hold the door pillar in alignment while the inside was bonded back together.

■ Where body sections are to be joined the surfaces must be keyed by sanding the areas that are to be fiberglassed. Then wiped down with acetone to further clean any impurities and aid adhesion.

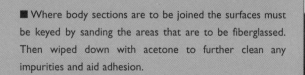
■ Strips of fiberglass cloth are bonded in place.

■ Prior to dismantling this door post looked structurally sound.

■ Once removed, it was evident that a new post should be fabricated.

■ Several previous attempts had been made at latch location and now repairs were needed to make these pillars sound again.

■ This is rectified by making sheetmetal formers that are screwed to the outer skin and fiberglassed from behind.

■ With the new door post fitted and all internal fiberglassing finished the door pillar shows the many modifications that have been made.

■ This area can be finished off with plastic filler, metal cover panels were also made and fitted.

■ After several layers are applied to the join the internal framing can be refitted.

■ The new framing is tied into the windshield posts before the front roof section is fitted.

■ This shot shows how the roof has grown and left a gap that must be filled. Aluminum is used and shaped to conform and join the two sections. Fiberglass will not adhere to the aluminum. Strips of cloth are cut to fit in this gap and glassed in place, as with the rear section. After curing, the aluminum is removed and glassed in from behind, where the rear sections are joined. This area is ground out with a 4" grinder and rovings (a rope type glass product) is fiberglassed in.

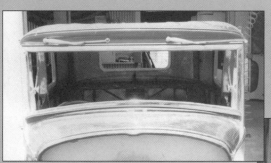

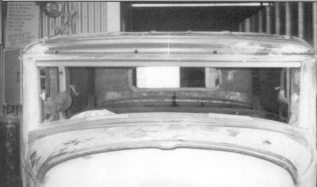

■ This front-on shot shows a stock windshield frame and a ribbed fiberglass roof insert. Both were retained and modified to suit the chopped roof. Compare this shot to the following one that shows the changed roof contour.

■ With the new steel roof bows fitted the roof insert is trial fitted and screwed in place.

■ To secure the insert, a fiberglass bonding agent or strips of cloth and resin are laid down. Sika Flex adhesive is applied to the roof bows and the insert is fitted and screwed down until the glass has cured.

■ With the screws removed, use a disc sander and sand an area one inch each side of the join and 1/8 inch below the gelcoat surface. Cut more strips of the cloth wide enough to bridge the joins and glass in place. As these reach the surface contours of the surrounding panels, glass tissue should be used to finish off. As the name implies it is a fine tissue consistency material. It will seal down the coarser fiber of the chopped strand mat and stop it from surfacing later in the paint finish. This bridging method is used on all joint areas.

■ The sections above the door opening where the roof was lengthened receive the same treatment as the insert, making the entire roof section much stronger than it was in original form.

■ This shot taken looking at the underside of the roof insert shows how the Sika Flex was use to glue the insert to the steel frame. As a result the body will feel solid and the roof won't "drum" as the car is driven down the highway.

■ Now that the basic chop is completed the vehicle can be pushed outside for a look at how the overall proportions have worked out.

■ All other body joins were treated the same way and a small amount of plastic filler is required to finish off the body contours.

■ Once the filler has cured and been sanded back the body is starting to shape up nicely. The roof section is almost ready for primer.

■ This particular body was manufactured in the early 1980s and supplied as an unframed body with the doors as inner frames and outer skins. The door halves as shown were not compatible with, nor did they conform to the outer body shape.

■ A previous owner had made an attempt at making an inner door frame to support the outer skin.

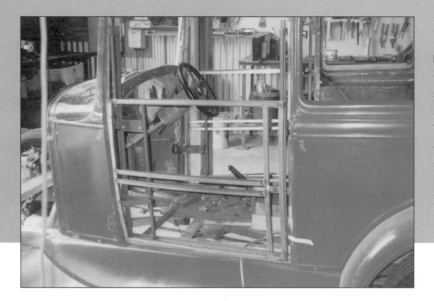

■ A new inner door structure was constructed taking into account the fitting of all modern internal mechanisms. This frame must conform closely to the body's outer shapes, as the door skin is to be bonded to it later.

■ The glass outer skin is chopped to suit the new body height.

■ The finished frames are powder coated. For protection against corrosion, as they will be concealed inside the door structure and will be susceptible to water through the window seals, as in all cars.

■ Hidden hinges and burst-proof door latches have been incorporated into the new door frames.

■ The chopped door skin is taped into place on the new door frames to check alignment when fitted to the body.

■ Sika Flex adhesive is used to bond the skin to the frame. Instructions on maximum efficiency of this material and safety requirements must be adhered to.

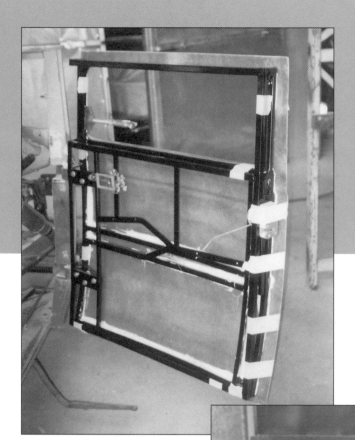

■ Once again Sika Flex is used to glue the skin to the frame and masking tape holds the skin in place while the adhesive cures. There should be no tension on the skin as an even gap is required between the frame and skin for maximum adhesion.

■ Before the inner skin is fitted the door latch operating mechanism and window winding gear is fitted.

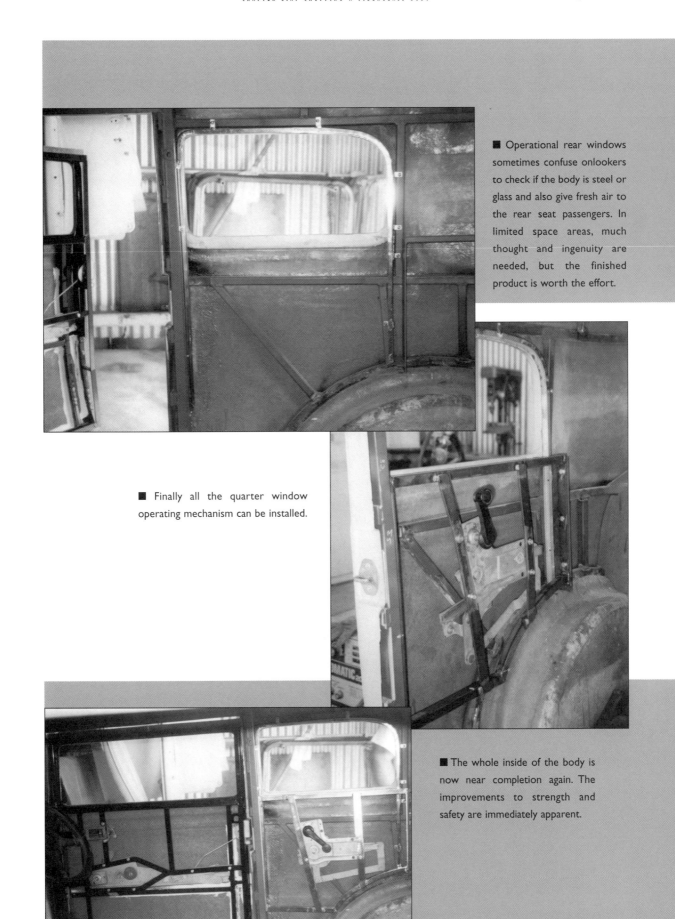

■ Operational rear windows sometimes confuse onlookers to check if the body is steel or glass and also give fresh air to the rear seat passengers. In limited space areas, much thought and ingenuity are needed, but the finished product is worth the effort.

■ Finally all the quarter window operating mechanism can be installed.

■ The whole inside of the body is now near completion again. The improvements to strength and safety are immediately apparent.

■ The top chop is completed and the repaired areas primed ready for the painting stages to begin. The profile of the body now has a decided "hot rod" flavor.

■ From the rear you would never know the entire roof was cut off this body and reattached three inches lower. The top chop is complete.

■ For comparison here's a stock bodied Model A Victoria. We like the chopped version better!

CHAPTER SEVEN
Steeling Out and Chopping a 1934 Ford Utility

HERE'S HOW TO REPLACE THAT old tired wood In a '34 Ford Ute with strong lightweight steel tube. Oh, and while we're at it, let's chop the top too!

The Floorpan: This Australian '34 Ford coupe utility was a complete body and chassis when originally obtained, but it was in very sad condition. These utes were different to most American based Fords of the era in that they had a predominantly wooden body frame rather than steel. While much of the original wood was still intact it was in very poor condition so the decision was made to replace it with steel. The body was removed from the chassis and disassembled after taking careful measurements of all the vital sections of wood. These measurements were transferred to the light box tube to make up a duplicate of the floor frame in steel. The steel used is 2-1/4 Inches by 1-3/8 inches and is very close to the original thickness of the Ford wood when laid on its broad side.

As each section of the floor frame was made up. It was clamped into position and each adjoining piece was clamped and tack-welded into place as we progressed. Once the complete floor frame was in position, measurements were checked, the whole assembly was completely welded and then measurements were checked again. It is important when working with this light box tube to make sure it is securely clamped before welding is carried out. It is very easy to work with, but does move around a lot with heat if not properly secured. The final step with the floor frame was to mark the chassis mounting holes, remove the frame from the chassis for drilling, and fit tubes into the holes to prevent the mounting bolts from squashing the box tube when tightened.

The Door Pillars: The outside edge of the doors and indeed the whole side of the body has a moderate curve from top to bottom. To duplicate this curve in the box tube would be quite a feat and one that's not really necessary. Instead, the pillar is made to conform with the Inner edge of the door, which simply has three straight sections to it roughly conforming to the outer curve. Once the sheet metal is attached to the pillar In Its curved shape, It will hold that shape anyway without any problems. When it comes time to mount the doors, heavy steel plates will be welded Into pillars to mount the hinges off.

Starting the ute Bed: The door pillars were welded into the body shell to hold that section fairly well in place while the ute bed section began to take shape from there. Firstly, an extra cross-tube was fitted on edge across the back of the floor frame and two duplicate cross-tubes were made up for the back end

of the bed. The ute bed, incidentally, is symmetrical front to back with the back edge of the doors which makes measurements and cross references easy. Two more tubes cut to length to run lengthways along the chassis and these five pieces were then assembled to form the basis of the ute bed floor. Note that the original rear ute bed mounts from the '34 were used to hold the new cross-tube. Next step was to make up the rear corner posts of the ute bed. These are in actual fact copies of the bottom half of the door pillars (remember we said the ute bed was symmetrical) except that they do have a slight curve towards the front of the car at their bottom edge. Top rails of the ute bed are straight forward lengths of tube, welded to the top of the rear corner pillars and the door pillars.

Chopping the top: Right from the start on this project, we intended to chop the top. Now that this basic frame of the ute bed was completed, and the body quite solid as a result, we turned to the top chopping part of the project. Final step was to carefully measure and mark, out the areas to be cut with special attention to how the pieces would have to fit back together. The rear section of the cab was cut first and back welded tack into place so that alignment could be  maintained as the rest of the chopping was carried out. The front section was next removed as was the top section of the door pillar.

Study the photos to see how we cut the rear edge of the front section so that there is only one cut going right through to the roof Insert area. The small amount of sheet-metal work left attached to the top of the door pillar was then removed to enable the pillar itself to be welded back in its shortened form. Next, the front section of the roof was welded back on after making sure to clean the original lead filler off the windshield posts, so that they can be welded back together easily. Finally, the

PART ONE

■ The floor frame is made up from sections of lightweight steel box tube to the same dimensions as the original wooden frame. Steel must be securely clamped while welding to prevent warpage. Note the rear ends of the frame have been tapered to follow the contours of the chassis rails.

small section of sheet-metal work was welded back into place at the top of the door pillar and strips of sheet-metal welded into the gap above the rear quarter window to complete the chopping operation.

Back to the ute bed: Now work turned back to a major part of the whole body rebuild. This involved the mounting bracketry for the rear guards, the tailgate area and other reinforcing members. Three extra uprights were welded in across the rear of the cab section to separate the cabin area from the ute bed area. The rear fender mounting brackets were made up from 3/4" square box tube rolled into the same shape as the fender and welded to the floor cross-tubes. Small pieces of flat strap were welded in between the rolled sections to provide mounting points for the fenders as shown in the photos. The final part of the operation is the tailgate area. First step here was to weld in a piece of tube between the tops of the rear corner pillars and then fit in two uprights to provide the basic tailgate opening. The top section of tube was then cut away to form the top of the tailgate itself. Hinges to be used will most likely be Holden ute items. Now that all the framework is complete, it's simply a matter of fitting all the original sheet-metal panels to the framework.

■ After marking the body mounting holes, the floor frame is removed for drilling. Small pieces of round tube are then inserted into the holes...

... and welded into place. A clean up with the grinder and the floor frame is ready to re-fit to the chassis. Now the mounting bolts won't squash the tube as they are tightened.

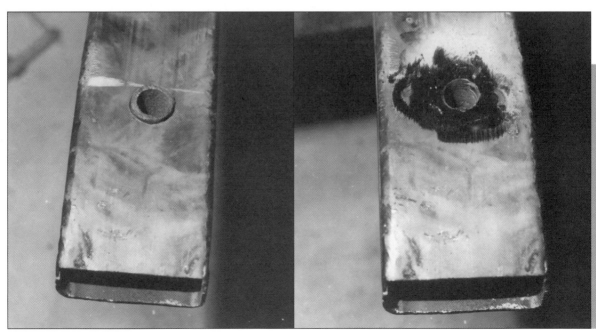

■ As the floor frame was finally welded, it was securely clamped in several positions to prevent heat warpage.

■ Door pillars conform to the shape of the inner edge of the door which has three straight sections. Once the outer sheet metal is attached to the pillar, it will retain its smooth curve from top to bottom.

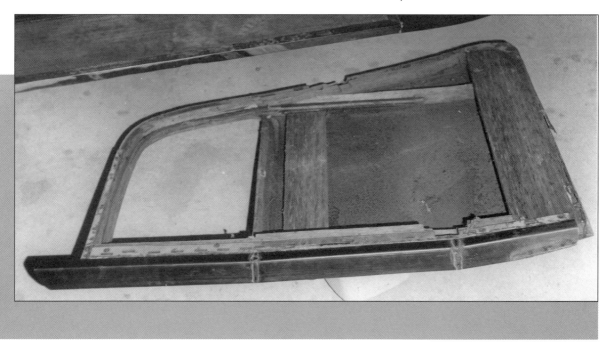

■ With the door pillars in place, the basic frame for the floor of the ute bed was fabricated. It uses the original rear floor mounts from the '34. The ute bed is symmetrical from front to rear.

■ Top rails of the ute bed attach to the rear corner posts and to the door pillars themselves. A cross-tube below the quarter windows ties the cab section together.

■ Now that the cab section was quite solid, we turned to chopping the top. Two inches were to be taken out from the areas as marked above. Note the shape of the cuts above the door pillar area.

■ The rear section was removed first and the two inch section cut out with a hack saw. Careful cutting and measuring makes for easier welding later.

■ The rear section was then securely tacked back into position right away so that the rest of the cabin could be used to check alignment before it too was chopped. Careful measuring ensures that the window openings line up again as they do here.

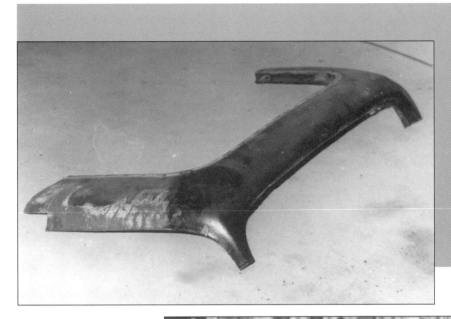

■ Now the front section is removed in one piece as shown. The stepped cut at the rear edge will make it easier to align that section when it is replaced.

■ This leaves only the top of the door pillar remaining at the original height. Already the quarter windows are taking on a squarer shape than original.

■ With the top of the door pillar removed, we have only a skeleton left. Because we replaced the rear section before the front was removed, we can now use It to keep the front pieces in alignment as they are refitted.

■ The small piece of bodywork was removed entirely from the top of the door pillar to allow the top of the pillar to be refitted and welded completely. Then the front section was welded back into place after cleaning all filler lead from the windshield pillars.

■ Three uprights across the back of the cabin separate it from the ute bed area. The body is now very strong but is much lighter than when the original woodwork was in place. Note how well the fender fits to its new bracketry.

■ Back to the ute bed where 3/4" box tube was used for the rear fender mounts. Four pieces of the tube were rolled to the same curve as the fenders and welded into the floor assembly. Tabs of flat strap tie the pieces together and provide mounting points for the fenders.

■ A trial fit of the original side skin shows that all is as it should be. Constructing the wheel arch brace and fender mounts in the manner shown means that the inner panel will be very easy to make and the fenderwell will have plenty of space for a big wheel and tire combination.

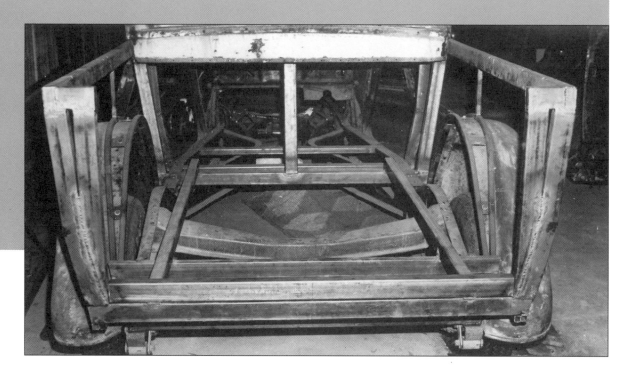

■ To fabricate the tailgate area a section of tube was first welded across top of the tailgate area and two uprights welded down to the base to leave a rectangular opening for the tailgate itself. The centre section of tube was then cut out and will be used to form part of the tailgate.

■ Final step in the top chopping exercise was to refit the small piece of bodywork to the top of the pillar and fill in the remaining gaps with pieces of sheet metal. That completes the top chop; the doors are next.

■ Now that the steel framework was 95% completed it was time for a quick mockup to see how the overall dimensions looked. Strength has obviously increased greatly with the fitting of the steel and the weight saving over the original wood is enormous. You can see here that the doors were chopped at the same points as their corresponding pillars and the top was lengthened in the middle.

■ At right is an Australian '32 Ford roadster door which also came from the factory with a wooden frame. We have replaced it with box tube steel curved to match the inner edge of the door and stitch welded in place.

■ Just for comparison here is a '34 Chevrolet coupe ute that has been steeled out in similar fashion to our '34 Ford. As with the Ford, the pickup bed is symmetrical from the doors rearward. The original Chevy inner fender wells appear to have been retained and incorporated into the new framework. Note the substantial members used to form the basis for the bed floor. This one will be able to carry a load.

■ Here's the same '34 Chevy ute in finished form. With steel framework replacing all that original wood this vehicle will last for many more years and stand up to the rigors exerted by more modern running gear. The vehicle will also weigh considerably less than it did in original form with all that wood now consigned to the fireplace!

GLOSSARY OF TERMS

■ "Work Harden"
The process whereby continual working on a piece of metal with hammer and dolly makes the material harder and more brittle. It eventually becomes difficult to form the metal into the required shape.
(See page 6.)

■ "Stretching"
The heat generated by welding can cause sheet metal panels to deform due to warpage. If this deformation is inwards on a convex panel the metal will need to be stretched to regain its original shape. Stretching is usually done by heavy hammering in the opposite direction to the deformation. Often this will need to be done to excess to "overstretch" the section concerned and then shrink it back to the original shape.
(See page 6.) (Also see "shrinking").

■ "Shrinking"
Heat generated by welding can also cause parts of the metal surface to deform above the surrounding metal. This high spot can be reduced by shrinking as described below. Excessive stretching can also be reduced by shrinking the high spots in the same manner. Large sheet metal panels will sometimes exhibit an "oil-canning" effect when slight pressure is applied to sections of the panel. This oil-canning can be removed by shrinking in the area concerned.

■ Shrinking high spots: The high spots are heated with an oxy-acetylene torch in spots about the same size as your thumbnail and only heated until glowing dull cherry red. Remove the heat and apply a cold wet rag or blast of compressed air to the area. You will be able to see it physically shrink to conform more to the surrounding area.

Use a slapping iron and dolly to take out the minor imperfections and blend into the surrounding area. The process may need to be repeated several times in the general area to achieve the desired result.
(See page 6 and also page 63 for pictorial explanation of stretching and shrinking.)

■ "Drip Rail" (or "rain gutter")
The gutter that runs around the roof to collect water in wet weather and prevent it from running into the tops of the doors. Some early vehicles don't have a gutter but in those instances usually had a horizontal ridge above the doors to divert the water away from the tops of the doors. The rain gutter is often formed when three sections of sheet metal meet together, being roof panel (or turret), side panels and the gutter itself.
(See page 9.)
(Also see "double skinned".)

■ "Hammer Welding"
The process sometimes used when joining sheet metal by butt welding in short sections and working the welded section with hammer and dolly while it is still glowing red. This process is used to minimise heat warpage from the welding.
(See page 15 and full explanation on page 28.)

■ "Double Skinned"
Auto manufacturers often join several panels together by overlapping them and using spot welders to fuse them together. Examples are rain gutters or drip rails, roof pillars and firewall installation.
(See door pillar example on page 19.)

■ "Worked"
Generally refers to working on a sheet metal panel using hammer or slapping iron and dolly to even out the surface after welding or dent repair has been undertaken. Also used to describe work done to realign body panels that don't quite align after modification.
(See page 20.)

■ "Turret"
Generally refers to that part of an automobile roof that extends above the drip rail or rain gutter.
(See page 31.)

■ "Rain Gutter"
See "Drip Rail" above.

■ "Roof Support Bows"
Most vehicles with a reasonably large roof area will incorporate strengthening support bows on the underside to give the roof rigidity and to prevent "drumming" from vibration as the vehicle is driven over rough surfaces. These bows are usuually spot welded to the roof rails inside the upper edge of the body and are installed under tension so that they exert pressure against the underside of the roof panel or "turret".
(See page 33.)

■ "Roof Rail"
Most vehicles incorporate a substructure where the "turret" joins to the rest of the vehicle body above the doors. Generally referred to as the roof rail it is usually a reinforced area that adds strength to the upper door area and provides a substantial anchor point for attaching the roof itself.
(See page 33.)

■ "Cut-off Wheel"

Most hand ginders and air drive tools will accept several different types of discs for different applications. Thicker examples are generally used for grinding and different combinations are used for metal, ceramic or masonry applications. Thinner discs are available for these grinders which are designed specifically for cutting purposes and again are available for metal, ceramic or masonry applications. These thinner discs should not be used for grinding. (See page 37.)

■ "Plug Welds"

Process used when a weld needs to be placed where there is no logical joining position. The example used in this book is where reinforcing tubes are placed inside a door pillar. The door pillar has holes drilled in it in several places to expose the tube inside. Plug welds are then used to weld up the hole and fuse it to the inner tube at the same time. (See page 40.)

■ "Dolly-off Method"

The most common method of panel beating is where the metal is sandwiched between the dolly and the impacting hammer so that the hammer blow is directed straight onto the dolly with the metal in between. The dolly-off method refers to some situations where the dolly is placed on a low spot and the hammer blows are aimed at the adjacent high spot so that the high and low surfaces are brought into the same plane. (See page 51.)

■ "Oil Canning"

After welding or dent repair a panel can become too flexible whereby pressure applied to the crown of the surface encourages it to flex inwards similar to the way an oil can does when pressed on the bottom. This is undesirable and should be removed, usually by shrinking. (See page 64.)

■ "Stitch Welding"

A method of welding used when adding reinforcement to another structure. Short welds are placed a small distance apart right along the edge of the sections to be joined together. (See page 95.)

■ "Fuse Welding"

This generally refers to a method used to join sheet metal panels together along a butted edge. The fit of the panels needs to be such that no, or very little, filler rod is used and the pieces of metal are simply fused together using the heat of an oxy-acetylene torch only. Normally the panels would be tack welded about every 3/4 inch first and then fuse welded from one end to the other in one continuous operation. (See page 97.)

■ "Butt Welding"

As above with fuse welding this method refers to joining two sections of metal together where the joining edges are butted together along their edges as distinct from being overlapped. (See page 113.)

■ "Keyed"

Refers to abrasive work being applied to a panel so that it leaves a surface that will enhance the ability of an adhesive (in this case fiberglass) to firmly grip the surface and hold. Usually this will require a slightly roughened surface rather than a very smooth surface. (See page 128.)

■ "Filler Lead"

Most body joins on older cars were filled smooth using body lead in much the same way that plastic or fiberglass fillers are used in more recent times. Common places where this lead was used is where the roof joins the main structure of the body at the windshield pillars and at the lower rear edge of the roof where it joins the quarter panels. The lead often needs to be completely removed to facilitate welding when a top is being chopped. (See page 150.)

FURTHER READING
SOME SUGGESTED TITLES

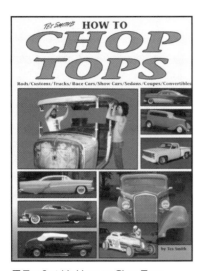

■ Tex Smith's How to Chop Tops.
By Tex Smith
Published by Hot Rod Library, Inc

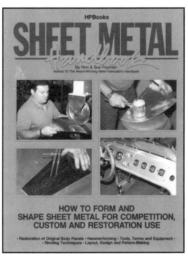

■ How to Chop Tops in 301 Photos.
By Tim Remus
Published by Motorbooks International

■ Ultimate Sheet Metal Fabrication.
By Tim Remus
Published by Wolfgang Publications

■ Metal Fabricator's Handbook.
By Ron and Sue Fournier
Published by HP Books

■ Sheet Metal Handbook.
By Ron and Sue Fournier
Published by HP Books

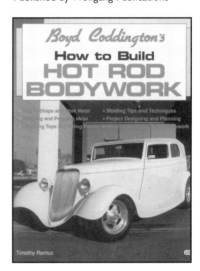

■ Boyd Coddington's How to Build Hot
Rod Bodywork.
By Tim Remus
Published by Motorbooks International

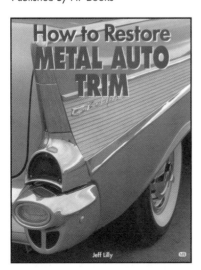

■ How to Restore Metal Auto Trim.
By Jeff Lilly
Published by Motorbooks International

■ Books available in Australia from Graffiti Publications (03) 5472 3805,
in New Zealand from Celebrity Books (09) 442 1046,
and in USA Classic Motorbooks 1 800 826 6600, www.motorbooks.com

GRAFFITI
Publications

Engineering Street Rods *by Larry O'Toole.*
How to go about building your own street rod using examples from existing rods. Based on engineering methods and principles known to be sound. It's one thing to build a street rod but it can be quite another to have it comply with current regulations and engineering requirements. How to minimise the hassles by using 100's of photos and diagrams to explain what is required. For the first time rodder or experienced builder there is plenty reference material to incorporate into your next project.

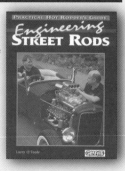

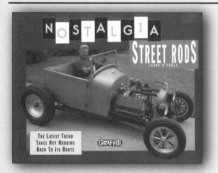

Nostalgia Street Rods
by Larry O'Toole.
Our latest full colour production featuring the best in nostalgia street rods from all around the world. 112 pages in landscape format so you get to see the cars at their best with concise, accurate information and no through the spine photos.

The Colourful World
by Larry O'Toole.
A landscape format publication to show rods at their best in full living colour. No "through the spine photos" or close ups of hubcaps, just large format, glorious colour photos of your favourite street rods with short captions giving you all the basic information about each car.

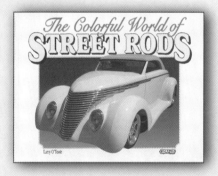

The Essential Holden V8 Engine Manual
by Larry O'Toole.
The Essential Holden V8 Engine Manual tells you everything you want to know about the Holden V8, from how to identify parts through to completely rebuilding an entire engine and stroker versions. An introduction tells you the story behind the design and development of the engine. Full specifications are included and you will also find extensive coverage of aftermarket involvement.

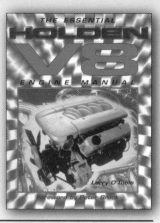

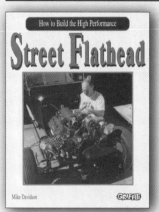

Street Flathead
By Mike Davidson.
This is the ideal book for the nostalgia hot rodder who seeks to power his or her street rod with a sweet running sidevalve. Everything you will ever want to know about building a high performance street flathead is contained in this book. A follow-up his best selling Flathead Fever book with another great title for flathead Ford fans.

Flathead Fever
By Mike Davidson.
Detail the methods and tricks Mike has used to build two versions of the Ford Flathead engine. One is mildly modified for increased performance in a street driven hot rod, with occasional outings to the drag strip, while the second is an all out race engine for the salt flats, where Mike's knowledge and ability with this engine has been proven with speeds in excess of 160 m.p.h.

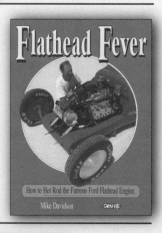

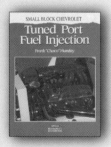

Small Block Chevrolet Tuned Port Fuel Injection
By Frank 'Choco' Munday
'Choco' Munday's experience really shows through with simple and logical, yet comprehensive detail. An extensive content list makes it very easy for the reader to quickly find the section dealing with any particular aspect of the TPI system. Combine this with extensive lists of diagrams, tables and photos and you have a very complete package that will impress even the most knowledgable Tuned Port Injection mechanic.

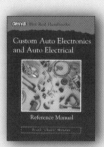

Custom Auto Electronics
By Frank 'Choco' Munday
Here's a book that tackles the electronic world in language that we can all understand and from a viewpoint of the hands-on enthusiast who wants to work with it on his own hot rod project. The book covers conventional wiring including the fitting of an entire loom into a hot rod type vehicle. Custom Auto Electronics and Auto Electrical Reference Manual is extensively cross-referenced to make your research easy.

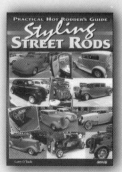

Styling Street Rods
by Larry O'Toole.
Here's a complete guide to styling your street rod using other rodders project vehicles as a guide. Ten chapters and over 300 photos give an insight as to how other rodders have designed all aspects of their street rod including front and rear end treatment, engine bays, access and vision, interiors, running boards and fenders and even accessories.

GRAFFITI PUBLICATIONS PTY LTD PO BOX 232 CASTLEMAINE 3450 VICTORIA AUSTRALIA
TELEPHONE: (03) 5472 3653 FACSIMILE: (03) 5472 3805
IN NEW ZEALAND CONTACT CELEBRITY BOOKS
TELEPHONE: (09) 442 1046 FACSIMILE: (09) 442 1047